CHINA 1966-1976,
CULTURAL REVOLUTION
REVISITED –
CAN IT HAPPEN AGAIN?

CHINA IN THE 21ST CENTURY

Additional books in this series can be found on Nova's website
under the Series tab.

Additional e-books in this series can be found on Nova's website
under the e-books tab.

FOCUS ON CIVILIZATIONS AND CULTURES

Additional books in this series can be found on Nova's website
under the Series tab.

Additional e-books in this series can be found on Nova's website
under the e-books tab.

CHINA 1966-1976, CULTURAL REVOLUTION REVISITED – CAN IT HAPPEN AGAIN?

GUANG WU

New York

For permission to use material from this book please contact us:
Telephone 631-231-7269; Fax 631-231-8175
Web Site: http://www.novapublishers.com

NOTICE TO THE READER

The Publisher has taken reasonable care in the preparation of this book, but makes no expressed or implied warranty of any kind and assumes no responsibility for any errors or omissions. No liability is assumed for incidental or consequential damages in connection with or arising out of information contained in this book. The Publisher shall not be liable for any special, consequential, or exemplary damages resulting, in whole or in part, from the readers' use of, or reliance upon, this material. Any parts of this book based on government reports are so indicated and copyright is claimed for those parts to the extent applicable to compilations of such works.

Independent verification should be sought for any data, advice or recommendations contained in this book. In addition, no responsibility is assumed by the publisher for any injury and/or damage to persons or property arising from any methods, products, instructions, ideas or otherwise contained in this publication.

This publication is designed to provide accurate and authoritative information with regard to the subject matter covered herein. It is sold with the clear understanding that the Publisher is not engaged in rendering legal or any other professional services. If legal or any other expert assistance is required, the services of a competent person should be sought. FROM A DECLARATION OF PARTICIPANTS JOINTLY ADOPTED BY A COMMITTEE OF THE AMERICAN BAR ASSOCIATION AND A COMMITTEE OF PUBLISHERS.

Additional color graphics may be available in the e-book version of this book.

LIBRARY OF CONGRESS CATALOGING-IN-PUBLICATION DATA

Wu, Guang.
  China 1966-1976, cultural revolution revisit : can it happen again? /
Guang Wu.
    p. cm.
  Includes bibliographical references and index.
  ISBN 978-1-62257-760-6 (soft cover)
  1. China--History--Cultural Revolution, 1966-1976--Causes. 2.
China--History--Cultural Revolution, 1966-1976--Influence. I. Title.
  DS778.7.W725 2011
  951.05'6--dc22
                                         2010049669

Published by Nova Science Publishers, Inc. † *New York*

Dedicated to my Beloved Parents
Qinghe Wu and Heqing Zhou

CONTENTS

PREFACE

Art is a lie that makes us realize the truth.

— *Pablo Picasso*

In 1993, I, as an STA (Science and Technology Agency, Japan) postdoctoral fellow, flew from Italy through Moscow to Japan. Before landing Japan, my personal view on Japan was totally and absolutely negative because of the second Sino-Japanese War (1937-1945). I could say that I had a hateful mood against Japan and Japanese people. However, I soon found my view on Japan and Japanese people at least out of date, if not biased, of course I was not brainwashed by any Japanese agent.

My experience in Japan leads me to wonder whether my view on many seemingly concluded issues is out of date, even biased. The first concluded issue running into my mind is the Chinese Cultural Revolution (1966-1976). Although my childhood went through the Cultural Revolution, my view on the Cultural Revolution was mainly based on what I read and what I was told. Honestly and frankly I did not use my brain to analyze the Cultural Revolution to reach my own conclusion

One day, a co-worker told me a fanny story about Russia in 90s of last century, based on my experience in Russia during that period, I should say that his story was a lie. However, his lie seemed to come from a newspaper report.

Perhaps, our view on history could be based on either deliberate or unintentional lies. In particular, our view on the Cultural Revolution is mainly based on painful stories, which popular writers repeatedly tell us again and again. Nevertheless these writers mainly are the Cultural Revolution survivals.

Frequently these writers underwent a deep personal or family tragedy during the Cultural Revolution. The number of these writers is not large, so why we, all the adults in China, could not conduct an analysis based on our own experience and ability, because all the adult people now living in China could be survivals or activists during the Cultural Revolution. This number is certainly far much larger than the number of popular writers, so why we do not trust our own analysis?

Along this line of thought, I try to duplicate all the problems in front of Mao Zedong before the Cultural Revolution, try to find the solutions to these problems, try to balance various powers during the Cultural Revolution, and so on and so forth.

To my surprise, my brain exercise and case study result in totally different conclusions from the seemingly conclusions on the Cultural Revolution. This book presents these brain exercise and case study on the Cultural Revolution.

Guang Wu   November 4, 2010
                                                          China

WHO'S WHO AND WHERE'S WHERE IN THIS BOOK

An Yuan – A district in city Pingxiang, province Jiangxi, China.

Cao Cao (155 AD – 220 AD) – A protagonist in classical Chinese novel, Three Kingdoms or Romance of Three Kingdoms.

Chen Lin (? – 217 AD) – The secretary to He Jin in classical Chinese novel, Three Kingdoms or Romance of Three Kingdoms.

Dan Ji – A beautiful lady, who was blamed for the collapse of dynasty Shang (1 600 BC— 1046 BC).

Deng Xiaoping (August 22, 1904 – February 19, 1997) – A Chinese leader, whose reform changes China.

Dong Zhuo – A protagonist in classical Chinese novel, Three Kingdoms or Romance of Three Kingdoms.

Fa Zheng – A protagonist in classical Chinese novel, Three Kingdoms or Romance of Three Kingdoms.

Gang of Four – Four high ranked officials during the Cultural Revolution including Jiang Qing (1915 – May 14, 1991, Mao Zedong's last wife); Zhang Chunqiao (1917 – April 21, 2005); Yao Wenyuan (1931 – December 23, 2005) , and Wang Hongwen (1935 –August 3, 1992).

Genghis Khan – Emperor of dynasty Yuan.

Han Wudi (156 BC – 87 BC) – An emperor in dynasty Han.

Hanzhong – A region in southwest of province Shaanxi, China.

He Jin (? – 189 AD) – A Regent Marshal under the last emperor of Dynasty Han in classical Chinese novel, Three Kingdoms or Romance of Three Kingdoms.

Hu Yaobang (1915 – April 15, 1989) – A former General Secretary of Chinese Communist Party.

Hua Guofeng (February 16, 1921 – August 20, 2008) – A former Chairman of the Communist Party of China and Premier of the People's Republic of China.

Huang Gai – A general in classical Chinese novel, Three Kingdoms or Romance of Three Kingdoms.

Lin Biao (December 5, 1907 – September 13, 1971) – A Chinese Marshal and the official heir to Mao Zedong.

Lin Liguo (1945 – September 13, 1971) – Lin Biao's son.

Liu Bang (256 BC – 195 BC) – The first emperor of dynasty Han.

Liu Bei – A protagonist in classical Chinese novel, Three Kingdoms or Romance of Three Kingdoms.

Liu Feng – A general in classical Chinese novel, Three Kingdoms or Romance of Three Kingdoms.

Liu Shaoqi (November 24, 1898 – November 12, 1969) – The 2nd Chairman of the People's Republic of China

Lu Xun（September 25, 1881 – October 19, 1936）– A Chinese writer, whom Mao Zedong praised frequently.

Mao Zedong (Mao Tse-tung; December 26, 1893 – September 9, 1976) – A former Chairman of Chinese Communist party.

Meng Da – A general in classical Chinese novel, Three Kingdoms or Romance of Three Kingdoms.

Mu Lan – A legendary heroine in dynasty North Wei (386 – 557).

Peng Dehuai (October 24, 1898 – November 29, 1974) – A Chinese Marshal.

Qin Shihuang (259 BC – 210 BC) – The first emperor of unified China.

Shangyong – A city in classical Chinese novel, Three Kingdoms or Romance of Three Kingdoms.

Shen Dan – Commander of the city, Shangyong, in classical Chinese novel, Three Kingdoms or Romance of Three Kingdoms.

Song Taizu (927 AD － 976 AD) – The first emperor of dynasty Song.

Tang Taizong (599 AD － 649 AD) – The first emperor of dynasty Tang.

Wang Ming (May 23, 1904 － March 27, 1974) – A senior leader of the early Chinese Communist Party

Wang Ping – A general in classical Chinese novel, Three Kingdoms or Romance of Three Kingdoms.

Xi Shi – A beautiful lady, who was blamed for the collapse of State of Wu.

Yan'an – A city in province Shaanxi, China.

Yuan Shao (? – 202 AD) – An imperial commander under the last emperor of Dynasty Han in classical Chinese novel, Three Kingdoms or Romance of Three Kingdoms.

Zhang Guotao (November 26, 1897 – December 3, 1979) – A founding member and leader of the early Chinese Communist Party.

Zhang Tiesheng – A Chinese student, who was famous for not being able to answer any single problem in university entrance examinations.

Zhaojun or Wang Zhaojun – A beautiful lady commissioned to marry a foreign prince for the peace between dynasty Han and Xiongnu.

Zhao Ziyang (October 17, 1919 – January 17, 2005) – A former General Secretary of the Chinese Communist Party.

Zhongnanhai – An area in central Beijing, China.

Zhou Enlai (March 5, 1898 – January 8, 1976) – The first Premier of the People's Republic of China.

Zhou Yu – A protagonist in classical Chinese novel, Three Kingdoms or Romance of Three Kingdoms.

Zhu De (December 1886 – July 6, 1976) – A Chinese Marshal and the founder of the Chinese Red Army.

Zhu Yuanzhang (October 21, 1328 – June 24, 1398) – The first emperor of dynasty Ming.

Zhuge Liang –A protagonist in classical Chinese novel, Three Kingdoms or Romance of Three Kingdoms.

Chapter 1

FUNDAMENTAL CONDITIONS
FOR OUR ANALYSIS

There are known knowns. These are things we know that we know. There are known unknowns. That is to say, there are things that we now know we don't know. But there are also unknown unknowns. These are things we do not know we don't know.

— Donald Rumsfeld, Former United States Secretary of Defense

The Cultural Revolution, which occurred between 1966 and 1976, is a particular chapter in Chinese history, not only because the Cultural Revolution is unique in the Chinese history but also because all the Chinese people, who underwent the Cultural Revolution, have an indescribable image buried in their memory. As the time goes on, this image fades and gives its place to new images occurred since then. However, the scar is still fresh for that generation of Chinese people, and any slight touch would cause the new pains.

Nowadays, the Cultural Revolution looks like an ancient legend for most Chinese people, because its meaning and significance appear simple. It was simple because many popular writers explained the Cultural Revolution in a very simple way.

Hence, one might ask why people should still continue talking and discussing the Cultural Revolution if it would be so simple? Still, why so many people died for such a simple Cultural Revolution, which was described as a family quarrel? As the Cultural Revolution was tragic not only for ordinary Chinese people but also for Mao Zedong himself because he lost the love of Chinese people, we should ask whether Mao Zedong was really so stupid as many writers considered to destroy his reputation completely? Actually we still can raise many questions regarding the Cultural Revolution.

All these questions mean that we need coolly examine the Cultural Revolution at the distance about a half a century. Besides, it would be far better for us to coolly examine ourselves at the distance between us and the events as well as the people to be analyzed before conducting our analysis on the Cultural Revolution.

1.1 WHO ARE WE?

We, the writers on Chinese Cultural Revolution that occurred about a half a century ago from 1966 to 1976, are certainly far away from the power center during that period of time. Otherwise we could not survive until this moment. In most cases, we were teenagers or in early childhood during that period of time, which means that we had not entered into the Chinese society yet, especially, we did not begin our journey along the career ladder during that period of time. The fact that we were so young during that period of time suggests that our memory, though it could be solidly buried deeply in our mind and brain due to any particular reasons, is not very much reliable and clear, but obscure.

Surely, some writers coming from the families, who were in the power center of China during the Cultural Revolution, but I really suspect if their parents could dare openly, honestly and frankly tell the real truth about the Cultural Revolution to their young children. Even they could dare do so, they still could not trust their children's ability to understand the complicity of Cultural Revolution. Actually, these parents might likely not know the true of cause for the launching of the Cultural Revolution.

Moreover the Chinese parents generally consider their business belonged to adults, not related to their children according to our Chinese tradition. This is particularly important because the Chinese tradition clearly distinguishes the children, even young men, from adults. This is to say, it is an extremely rare case that parents can openly, honestly and frankly tell what they are doing, what they are planning to do, what their conspiracy is, etc. In general, children know little, if none, about what their parents do, about their social positions, about their job duties, even about their life in the past, and so on and so forth.

Doubtless, this Chinese tradition could efficiently and effectively prevent any children from obtaining the real insights into what was really happened in the power center although some writers might claim to have the knowledge on the power center.

Of course, we could not exclude the possibility that some parents from the power center dared tell their children the real stories, however, this possibility was still doubtfully slim to throw any real light onto what happened in the power center, because most parents were extremely busy spending their full days engaged in various meetings and activities during the Cultural Revolution. It was the common phenomenon during the Cultural Revolution that parents could be absent from home for months, therefore what these parents could tell would be the most impressed issues occurred to them rather than a full picture. Even, they wanted to tell the whole picture, it was not possible to condense a day-long, week-long, month-long and year-long picture into reasonable conversations in a short time. Yet we do not mention the fact that their brains physically did not have such large memory to remember all occurred events, even they might have written diary everyday. Thus, what in our minds and our previous generation's minds is a fraction of knowledge about the Cultural Revolution.

In short, all these factors strongly impair our ability as writers to analyze the Cultural Revolution fairly and objectively, needless to say other factors.

On the other hand, we are also readers of Chinese Cultural Revolution, because we at last have read something about the Cultural Revolution, more importantly we ourselves have read many required materials during the Cultural Revolution. Very similarly, I would guess that all the readers are equally far away from the power center during the Cultural Revolution. What a reader reads would either confirm her/his personal view on the Cultural Revolution or provide additional knowledge and background information about the Cultural Revolution.

Therefore, unless we would write something like memoirs about the Cultural Revolution, otherwise we analyze the issue that we do not know how much we do not know.

1.2. WHOM WE TRY TO ANALYZE?

It is Mao Zedong, who then held the title of Chairman of Communist Party and initiated the Cultural Revolution, or Great Cultural Revolution, or

Great Proletarian Cultural Revolution. Hence, one cannot avoid analyzing Mao Zedong if she/he would like to address or analyze the Cultural Revolution.

No one can deny the cool and real fact that any comparison between Mao Zedong and us, writers and readers alike, will humble us enormously, in despite of any standards and criteria. Equally importantly, we would not feel much better in comparison with all the associates surrounded Mao Zedong in most cases. The implication is very clear: we are powerless and have never tasted the joy and sufferings Mao Zedong had when he held unlimited power, we never have the panorama appeared in front of Mao Zedong, and so on and so forth.

More scientifically and psychologically, we can never understand the origination of Mao Zedong's decision, even worse, we can never guess correctly out anything that occurred in Mao Zedong's mind. In scientific terms, it evidently means that we are trying to analyze what happened inside a black box, at the best we have only the inputs and outputs, then we try to build the relationships between inputs and outputs, and what happened led to build these relationships.

Still, we must frankly and honestly admit that the mental activities in our minds are not as complicated and sophisticated as those in Mao Zedong's mind, and the pathway of our mental activities would not be the same as, even similar to the pathway undergone in Mao Zedong's mind.

An ancient Chinese proverb may apply to us: "To evaluate noble people's activity with a mean person's mind", yi xiao ren zhi xin du jun zi zhi fu, in Chinese pronunciation. Cannot we say what we are doing is this type of work?

It is also said that one cannot value others if she/he does not have similar experience and background. No one can reverse the time, thus no writers would have similar experience and background as Mao Zedong had.

1.3. CAN WE TRUST HISTORY?

A sorry and sad fact is that history is progressively and inevitably becoming a toy, which everyone can play for her/his own purposes, mostly for entertainments as well as moneymaking. On the other hand, it is oftentimes said that let history judge whether or not a certain event is right. This saying implicitly implies that it is only the historians who can clarify the underlined reason of certain historical event, give the contemporary meanings to these historical events, and then award credits to historical figures.

However, I am not quite certain whether the historians have such an ability to do this job properly and correctly because each individual can read only a tiny fraction of history in her/his life span, especially in this information abundant era. Consequently if a historian could draw the conclusion based on these fractions of history he reads, it could be a heavily biased and unreliable personal view.

Besides, another pitiful fact is that the historical documents might not be available to historians. In addition, a very interesting fact to be considered is whether we can trust the historical media, not only because there were censorships for many medias but also because medias frequently enlarger the meanings of a simple fact and modify what really happened. These scaling and modifications seem to be a common practice. Actually, can we trust the current medias, which will be the historical documents in future?

Moreover, as a scientific researcher myself, I know very well that a researcher prefers to write the articles, which the ordinary people cannot understand, in order to publish them in purely prestigiously academic journals. Thus, I would presume that the similar phenomenon prevails in the research field of history, i.e. the historians would have the trend to write their analyses for prestigious research journals with high impact factors, but get no public attentions.

For this reason, the description and analysis of history leave to the hands of popular writers, who write various historical stories as well as biographies according to their imaginations, their knowledge and their research. These popularly historical stories and biographies arguably are the history we are familiar with. That is why the history is in need to be reassessed, because the accounts are confused and contradictory, in particular the Chinese history was heavily manipulated either intentionally or unintentionally.

1.4. POSSIBLE BIASES IN OUR ANALYSIS

Although the Cultural Revolution occurred almost a half a century ago, currently most Chinese adults still have a living memory because we are still surviving. This could theoretically construct the first bias in our analysis because the Cultural Revolution has changed the fates and lives of so many Chinese people, how many new hopes and dreams appeared during the Cultural Revolution, and how many hopes and dreams were brutally crushed later on. Thus, unavoidably the personal emotion, feeling, suffering and hatreds would mix with our analysis. Although the personal suffering and family pains should be an important aspect during the Cultural Revolution, it does not represent the very real nature of Cultural Revolution. This is so because no one could imagine that the initial aim of Cultural Revolution was to torture each and every ordinary Chinese citizen. If this would be the initial aim, then this aim is certainly different from the aim defined by almost all the current accounts on the aim of the Cultural Revolution.

The second bias would be the different views between the time of analysis of Cultural Revolution and the time of occurrence of Cultural Revolution, or the different views between now and then. Notwithstanding the fact that many people currently considered the Cultural Revolution irrational and negative, it should have sufficient and enough reasons to conduct the Cultural Revolution in China. Otherwise, this Cultural Revolution would not be possible to occur or died immediately after its beginning. The historical fact was that the majority of Chinese people were actively involved in the Cultural Revolution with greatest enthusiasm, and it was no doubt that the Cultural Revolution was bright for that majority of Chinese people, and gave the hopes and dreams, and of course pains and suffering to almost each Chinese people eventually. This historical fact was particularly important because the Cultural Revolution was a massively political movement involved thousands of millions of Chinese people, for such a size of massively political movement, it would be extremely hard to conduct without the support of thousands of millions of ordinary Chinese people. On the other hand, we can easily raise an example how the ordinary Chinese people were passively and successfully resistant to Mao Zedong's policy during the Cultural Revolution: this resistance would be related to the policy "Down to the Countryside Movement", which lost its strong momentum almost immediately, and lost its effect merely within very few years.

The third bias is whether we can use our current view to analyze the history. This argument is similar to the problem of whether the German people can apply the West Germany laws to the German people who did "wrongs" during their lifetime in the former East Germany.

Nevertheless, these biases impede our ability to analyze the Cultural Revolution critically and objectively. This suggests that we may not be able to evaluate and value Mao Zedong's Cultural Revolution correctly and unbiased.

1.5. WHO CAN PERFORM THE ANALYSIS?

It is very likely that there are more writers who write historical stories than the historians who write historical stories, thus we can generally read more understandable stories on history than serious historical articles and books.

This book will not deal with endless sufferings and pains in individuals during the Cultural Revolution, but try to analyze the Cultural Revolution at national level. This is so because it is only to do the analysis at national level, we can get a full picture on the Cultural Revolution.

In scientific literature, particular the US research journals, it is required to disclose the financial support and conflict of interests in order to avoid unnecessary bias in studies. Similarly, we, the writers on the Cultural Revolution, should do our best to avoid any possible bias due to family sufferings, interruption in personal career, lost of fortune, personal feelings, etc. Without these, anyone could analyze the Cultural Revolution objectively rather than subjectively.

1.6. OUR APPROACH FOR ANALYSIS

Taking all the above arguments into consideration, we could minimize various weakness and shortages if we could understand what we were about to do in the similar situation as Mao Zedong was then. In other words, we should try to make decisions as if we were in Mao Zedong's position.

This could be at least a brain exercise or case study to see whether we, the ordinary Chinese people, could solve the problems faced in front of Mao Zedong through different ways and means. Perhaps, in this way, we can safely and comfortably analyze Mao Zedong and his Cultural Revolution.

Even the analysis along this way, we still must frankly admit another fatal weakness in ourselves, that is, we cannot produce the particular thoughts and ideas that Mao Zedong produced at that time.

Within above arguments in mind, we could be able to minimize our potential mistakes in analysis.

Therefore, our analysis will not rely on one or two sentences from a personal history, from any interesting anecdotes, from a personal memoir, and from a secret channel. This is so simply because (i) one or two sentences cannot change our historical course, (ii) the anecdotes can color the history but cannot replace the cool judgments and decisions, (iii) the personal memoirs would sometimes decay this serious history into an ordinary family life with love affairs, and (iv) no secret agent had so far got any important documents, which would have the impact as similar as the publication of secret report in Twentieth Party Congress of Soviet Communist Party.

On the other hand, the popular historical stories do not need to put the writers and readers in front of problems in history, while we will try to do these things in this book. Therefore, we should try to recreate all the circumstances, and then we would try our best to logically deduce what to do based on the black box with inputs and outputs, actually we even do not have all the inputs as their correct sequential along the historical time course.

Hence, the question is about: can we, the ordinary Chinese people, make a similar decision based on the balance between advantage and disadvantage? In this way, our analysis would be somewhat similar to a brain exercise and case study.

Chapter 2

PROBLEMS EXISTED BEFORE THE CULTURAL REVOLUTION

History may not be a very practical study, but it teaches some useful lessons, one of which is that nothing is accidental, and that if men move in a given direction, they do so in obedience to an impulsion as automatic as is the impulsion of gravitation.

— *Brooks Adams, The Theory of Social Revolutions [1]*

Since the beginning of 20th century, the role, which the Chinese statesmen and national leaders played, has been significantly different from the statesmen and national leaders before 20th century. In feudal Chinese society, the statesmen and national leaders held the power on the assumption that the country belonged to their family. Their daily job was highly likely to connect with the civil justice if they would like to be active in the national life and their duty. So these statesmen and national leaders, emperors, played a role somewhat similar to judges.

Since the beginning of 20th century, the leaders got their power and lofty positions on the assumption that these leaders would bring a better life for ordinary people and would make each personal richer and happier under their government rather than under previous governments. This promise changed the role of national leaders from civil judges to "businessmen", "engineers", "educators", etc.

This was particularly true for the revolutionary leaders because they overthrew the old governments completely on the promise that they would bring not only the hope for a better life but also the real better life to very ordinary people.

Mao Zedong's revolution, which led to the creation of the People's Republic of China, was indeed totally and entirely different from all previous peasant revolutions, although the basic forces for Mao Zedong's revolution were still very common Chinese peasants. This radical difference lays that any previous peasant revolution would build a new dynasty with the same social structure, same social hierarchy, and the same administrative system used in previous feudal dynasties. Even, the most modern peasant revolution in Chinese history, Taiping Heavenly Kingdom, which was under the cover of Christian belief, it still adopted almost all the old social systems left from generation to generation. These old styled revolutions in the Chinese history promised a little, if not none, to thousands of millions of peasants.

One important promise in Mao Zedong's revolution was to give the land to each ordinary peasant. Of course, there were still many other promises or plans, such as to give a better life to ordinary Chinese people, to give a free education to ordinary Chinese people, to give a free medical treatment to ordinary Chinese people, to give a job to each person, and to give a comfortable retirement life to elder people. Likely, these are the promises and plans for each revolution, even for each new leader. So, we perhaps could expend this observation to the leaders in other nations around the world.

How to materialize these promises and plans would be the greatest and basic problem existed before the Cultural Revolution.

2.1. PROBLEMS WORTHY MENTIONING

The creation of the People's Republic of China was totally based on the completely different new concepts, thus almost all the social systems and social structures existed until then were abandoned. This perhaps was the natural result for China in 20th century because several social systems coexisted parallel, i.e. feudalism, capitalism, colonialism and socialism before the creation of the People's Republic of China.

The promises and plans literally would render the life styles for the new Chinese leaders very different from the leaders in previous peasant revolutions. In the past, the newly crowned peasants would stay in power literally doing nothing because the feudal economy did not require many interventions either from the new dynasty or from the overthrown dynasty, the new peasant-become emperor simply gave different titles and different size of lands to the people, who contributed to their revolutions, and then stayed well for the rest of their life if they succeeded to destroy all the enemies of previous dynasty.

Thus, the problem for the People's Republic of China would be a completely new problem because even the democratically elected leader would still have the inherited administrative system to manage the daily life. From this point of view, perhaps it was potentially good for the Chinese Communist Party to struggle for 28 years to get national power because Mao Zedong and his fellow-comrades should have enough experience to operate their administrative systems from small scale to national scale. Accordingly, the creation of the People's Republic of China was not entirely from zero, because Mao Zedong and his fellow-comrades already had millions of cadres to work for this new country at various levels.

These millions of cadres mainly came either from the Chinese army, People's Liberation Army (PLA) or from revolutionary students or underground Chinese Communist Party members, etc. They since then began to operate all the administrative affairs on daily bases, and factually became the career'officials. Nevertheless, the job to accomplish the plans designed by Mao Zedong and his fellow-comrades was mainly on these cadres' shoulders.

These career officials as we will see in Chapter 3 would be the main targets of the Cultural Revolution when we look back the history of the Cultural Revolution. In such a case, it could argue that these career officials or career bureaucrats were themselves a problem existed before the Cultural Revolution.

One problem needed to mention here would be the Korean War. The Korean War, although China appeared to be a winner in fighting against the US troops and stopped their advance, was in fact no winner, especially for China. This was so because the pre-war state remains until today. Worse than that, the US troops obtained the right to permanently station in the South Korea while the Chinese troops had returned back to the Chinese territory. If we compare the Korean War with Vietnam War, the Korean War was not successful for each party. Arguably, China after sacrificing so many lives and spending so much money gained little in Korean War compared with the US, meanwhile Japanese economy rapidly developed during the Korean War.

Another problem would be what type of state China should become, for most of Chinese leaders had very little experience abroad, so what they saw during their life was mixed but corrupted social systems either under the Kuomintang (Nationalist Party) governance or under Japanese governance or under local warlord's governance. Still, not many Chinese leaders mastered the foreign languages, so they did not have up-dated knowledge on the

Marxism and Leninism that they followed. For many Chinese leaders, what type of China they should build was an open question, perhaps for Mao Zedong himself. This argument could be proved by the fact that Zhou Enlai tried to shake hand of the U.S. Secretary of State, John Foster Dulles, in 1954, which meant that China had the intention not only to follow the Soviet path but also at least to be interested in the US. In particular, the question of whether China would become an industrial country or agricultural country seemed to be important. This question could be possibly reasonable not only because most Chinese leaders came from countryside and the majority of Chinese were peasants at that time, but also because the international communism could advocate the agricultural country for a period of time as we have seen that Khmer Rouge tried to change Cambodia into a commune agricultural country at their early stage of controlling of Cambodia.

A serious problem for the new China was that almost all the Chinese leaders during that period had rich experience in wars, and had less experience in economic development. This argument can be verified by analysis on the approaches of Chinese economic development from 1949 to 1966. During that period of time, China has adopted several different policies, even sometimes opposite and contradictory policies. Clearly, not only China as a nation but also Chinese leaders as administrators sought the ways to build China, or to accomplish their promises and plans. For example, at first, China tried to cooperate with the Soviet Union, whose aids helped China to build the base for Chinese industrial development, but the cooperation stopped due to various reasons.

After creation of People's Republic of China, the urban population actually became an unbearably economic burden to the Chinese government. This was so because the government assigned each person, who from birth to death had a permanent residence in city, a quote of food in form of coupon. This was indeed a privilege for people living in cities, because the residents in rural areas were not entitled this quote of food. In fact this privilege included many unworkable people in cities.

2.2. PROBLEMS SOLVED

Although we mentioned problems existed before the Cultural Revolution, which could be regarded as unsolved problems, we could now turn our attention to the solved problems. However, arguably when the mankind solves a single problem, they might also create several new problems originated from the previous solution, but the mankind may not know that they create several new problems at the time when they are trying to solve a single problem.

The first solved problem would be how to deal with the millions of Chinese troops, who overthrew the Kuomintang government, as we know that there is always a problem in disbanding the army after a big war as we read [2]:

> "In the mean time, the Parliament, having finished the war, were ready to disband the army. But the army did not wish to be disbanded. They would not be disbanded. The officials knew very well that if their troops were dismissed, and they were to return to their homes as private citizens, all their importance would be gone. There followed long debates and negotiations between the army and the Parliament, which ended, at last, in an open rupture. It is almost always so at the end of a revolution. The military power is found to have become too strong for the civil institutions of the country to control it."

In Chinese feudal history, the marshals and generals had only two ways to conduct their future life after overthrowing of the old dynasty: (i) to retire from public life and live somewhere luxuriously, and (ii) to become a subordinate in a civil local administration. In any case, there was no possibility for them to become warlords. For ordinary Chinese soldiers, this did not seem to be a problem because the Chinese people far more enjoy family life, these soldiers were very glad to return home.

Mao Zedong's way towards this problem was really different from previous feudal dynasties, Mao Zedong made the Chinese marshals as ministers in major ministries, high ranked generals as ministers in minor ministries, and almost all the officers in Chinese army finally had a civil position in various local administrations, but they generally did not work under previous civil officials because they themselves became chief civil officials. This way indeed solved a headache problem, but created new problems, mainly, these army officers after becoming career officials knew very little how to develop the Chinese economy, and also created an entire generation of career bureaucrats.

The most important promise to millions of peasants during the Chinese civil war was to redistribute the ownerships of farmlands in China. This problem was almost immediately solved as the People's Liberation Army went on. However, this redistribution of land also created the new problem, which could be seen in other countries such as Zimbabwe in the early 21st century. The particular problem for China was that although the ownership of farmlands changed hands, the results were almost the same because this land still could not feed the increased population with unparallel increased demand for better life. Anyone, who has a chance to visit the rural area in mountain area in China, would easily get such a conclusion, that is, the change of ownership does not mean the increase of productivity. This is so because the severely natural environments, poor roads and poorly educated farmers cannot radically increase the agricultural output. Nevertheless, the difficulty in feeding the increased population after changing of ownership could be the basic and main reason leading to the creation of People's Commune.

Perhaps, the most headache problem was how to make China become an industrial country. This was particularly difficult because most Chinese leaders had sufficient experience in agriculture, but little experience in industry. Perhaps, this was one important reason of why Liu Shaoqi had more to say because he at least had more experience with industrial workers. The way to solve this problem was to cooperate with the Soviet Union, which helped China to build the necessary infrastructure for Chinese industry. Of course, the Chinese leaders also applied their traditional methods, which they were very familiar with, to speed up the process of industrialization; for example, Mao Zedong initiated a movement, which was very similar to a political movement, to increase the output of steel that finally failed.

At international level, the big problem was how to let the People's Republic of China be recognized. This problem was partially solved with the incorporation to the socialist countries, but failed after the cooling of relationship between China and USSR.

These partially solved problems strongly re-emerged in various ways to become new problems after 3-year long natural disasters, which raised the serious question about the ways that national leaders led China to go along with since the creation of People's Republic of China.

2.3. LOSERS, CONTROLLING AND TURNING POINTS

With the sharp difference between the high expectations from both people and leaders and the difficulties encountered in developing the new China, there must be some losers at different levels. The common sense and knowledge suggest us that the time between 1963 and 1966 could be the time for Chinese leaders to find the scapegoats and regrouped their power and force, because we could divide the time between 1949 to 1966 into several phases: (i) the first phase would be the greatest joy and happiness because the Chinese Communist Party had struggled for 28 years to create the People's Republic of

China, (ii) the second phase would be the time of Korean War, (iii) the third phase would be that all the national leaders concentrated on economic development after Korean War, and so on and so forth. Frankly and honestly, the Chinese leaders made many great efforts to improve the life of ordinary people during the third phase.

During the first three phases, arguably there were fewer losers and scapegoats, because the nation was advancing with new hope although China and the Chinese people experienced many events and some very difficult periods of time.

However, the series of failures naturally produced losers and also required scapegoats, the Chinese history before 1966 shows that the only permanent loser was the Chinese Marshal, Peng Dehuai, because he could no longer form strong groups to initiate the power struggle at very high level, while Mao Zedong was definitely a temporary loser because he still could form strong groups of supporters to initiate the Cultural Revolution at a very near future.

The process to find losers was in fact quite difficult because the Chinese philosophy advocates harmony and teamed responsibility, therefore it would be arguable to say that there were few losers in Chinese society and history.

On the other hand, it would be easy to find the scapegoats although there were some real perpetrators. Most of scapegoats were the so-called class enemies, of course, some of these indeed played very bed roles, but their political power and influence were completed limited after defeating of Kuomintang (Nationalist Party) in Mainland China. However, the class enemies could serve as a good pretext to launch a purge, however as we will see that the Cultural Revolution was not this type of purge aiming at class enemies (also see Section 3.1, Chapter 3).

Now we should ask whether there was or were a single or several controlling points, at which the Chinese people or Chinese leaders could stop launching of the Cultural Revolution. This hypothesis is unlikely to be true, namely, there was no controlling point before the Cultural Revolution to prevent the Cultural Revolution from launching. This was so because the Chinese leaders and Chinese people demanded an explanation for the failures in accomplishing the promise of better life. This demand would particularly be stronger among Chinese leaders than in ordinary Chinese people, not only because there were few ways to express the people's opinion but also the Chinese people were less educated in those years. In fact, it was Mao Zedong, who held the power to control the course where China was going forwards, so the fact that he retreated from the first position did not mean that Mao Zedong lost all his control. Thus, the time that Mao Zedong's lost of power could not be considered as a controlling point, which could prevent the Cultural Revolution from launching.

Perhaps, the demand for an explanation for the failures in building of new China was a turning point, from which China was going along the way to do something either for clarifying her past failures or for defining new efforts for the future.

2.4. ALTERNATIVE APPROACHES

The Chinese people, mainly post-rationalists and armchair commentators, frequently question the historical figures whether these historical figures could do something different to avoid the historical catastrophes and blame the historical figures selfish and stupid to make some selfish and stupid decisions, which can now be viewed as irrational and foolish. Unfortunately, we could neither hear the explanations from these historical figures nor see the results from alternative approaches. Still, the post-rationalists and armchair commentators make such accusations mainly based on their own short-term reflection and meditation on the disastrous results.

However, I would suggest that the history could have only one pathway, which was what we see now. The historical figures perhaps were less impetuous and less unwise than most post-rationalists and armchair commentators imagined. The historical figures might have many chances to consult with many clever and prudent people rather than many post-rationalists and armchair commentators made the accusations based on their personal experience and reflection on aftermath without any consultation.

There is indeed a branch of fiction called alternative history [3], but it belongs to a genre of fiction. Sometimes I feel that the Chinese post-rationalists might have mixed the real history with the fictionally alternative history.

History seems to suggest that the decisions made by the historical figures appeared to be the only solution after carefully balancing various factors, and the decisions were painful results after intensive discussions or repeatedly personal weighing of various factors and facts. These decisions appeared to be no-other-choice decisions after exhausting all other possible ways. For example, the US government did her best to avoid her involvement in World War II, and the no-other-choice decision was made only after the attack from Japanese army on the Pearl Harbor.

However, we could still try to analyze whether there were alternative approaches to solving the problems existed before the Cultural Revolution.

The most visibly alternative approach would be that Liu Shaoqi would still have held the power, and continued his policy in countryside. However, I would suggest that Liu Shaoqi's policy could be less radical and effective than Deng Xiaoping's reform, which still took 20 years, even 30 years to change China. By any standard, Liu Shaoqi's policy was far much weaker than Deng Xiaoping's reform, thus Liu Shaoqi's policy might not lead China to change very much radically. Actually, this alternative approach would do a little to change anything with respect to the Chinese career bureaucratic system, international affairs, and other unsolved problems. Of course, Liu Shaoqi's policy might lay the foundation for Deng Xiaoping's reform. If so, arguably this alternative approach would serve China better. However, an unsolved problem for Deng Xiaoping's reform would be how Deng Xiaoping could get the support from hard lined leaders, while the Cultural Revolution wiped out most leaders no matter whether they are hard lined or soft lined, leftists or rightists. Another problem with this alternative approach would be whether Deng Xiaoping could reach the position of national leader? This is so because there were many senior leaders ahead of Deng Xiaoping along the career ladder. However, how China would have the reform if Deng Xiaoping would not be able to reach the top position?

Another possibly alternative approach would be a Cultural Revolution at a far smaller scale. In some sense, the Socialist Education Movement (Four Cleanups Movement) taking place from 1963 to 1966 could be considered as a small scaled Cultural Revolution, because it mainly focused on class struggle that will soon be furthermore strengthened during the Cultural Revolution. Thus, the question for this alternative approach would be whether the Socialist Education Movement could continue for a longer period in a nationwide scale?

The above two alternative approaches in some sense could be workable, at least theoretically. There could be some unimaginable approaches, which are not only totally theoretically impossible but also practically unworkable. For example, the democratic election could be alternative approach, however not only the Chinese people had no such tradition but also the Chinese society did not have such a mechanism. Similarly, the Deng Xiaoping's reform was also unworkable during that period of time.

Honestly and frankly we should say by now that we already exhausted our ideas no matter whether our ideas were workable or unworkable as alternative approaches to solve the problems existed before the Cultural Revolution.

Chapter 3

MAO ZEDONG'S OPTIONS AND PREPARATIONS

Right, as the world goes, is only in question between equals in power, while the strong do what they can and the weak suffer what they must.

— *Thucydides (c. 460 BC – c. 395 BC), The History of the Pelopon-nesian War [4]*

After stating and analyzing the problems and situations before the Cultural Revolution, let us look at all possible options, which we can now think out, in Mao Zedong's hands.

As the Cultural Revolution is a revolution, it suggests the following circumstances: (i) Mao Zedong should have some strong enemies, whom the revolution is directed; (ii) Mao Zedong had no other options to remove these enemies except for the Cultural Revolution; and (iii) Mao Zedong wanted to change the social systems, which have no other ways to be changed except for the Cultural Revolution.

It was very unlikely that Mao Zedong launched the Cultural Revolution for passing his power on to his heir or for his relatives not only because he had no suitably direct heirs, but also Mao Zedong was in a weakened position after his failures with little real power in his hands to do so.

Thus, the question is how Mao Zedong could balance the advantages against the disadvantages through his options if he would launch the Cultural Revolution.

As a deep thinker and broad strategist, Mao Zedong should also make serious preparations for the Cultural Revolution rather than did a simple mental work. This should be why Mao Zedong did not launch the Cultural Revolution immediately after losing his power in day-to-day state managements. Nevertheless, the key and critical principle in Mao Zedong's considerations was not to furthermore lose his power in case that the whole country would go into chaos as well as other unfavorable situations.

3.1. WHO IS MAO ZEDONG'S ENEMY?

Many popular stories and analyses either implicitly or explicitly indicated that Liu Shaoqi was Mao Zedong's number one enemy because Liu Shaoqi held the position of State Chairman, which forced Mao Zedong to be retreated from day-to-day affairs of state and governance [5]. However, anyone with a little bit knowledge on the contemporary Chinese history would agree that Mao Zedong was almost always free from the routine day-to-day affairs simply because he was a thinker and a strategist. Therefore, the conflict between Mao Zedong and Liu Shaoqi could not be considered as the main cause for initiation of Cultural Revolution. And such a consideration oversimplified the very complicated facts and factors.

Still, the Cultural Revolution would have finished far much earlier than 10-year long duration if Liu Shaoqi would be Mao Zedong's only political rival because Liu Shaoqi died at very early stage of the Cultural Revolution, therefore their conflict and dispute would be settled and sealed immediately after Liu Shaoqi's death. Thereafter there would be no more reasons to conduct the Cultural Revolution.

Perhaps, the prevailing of such assumption that the Cultural Revolution was launched to eliminate Liu Shaoqi could be attributed to the common sympathy on the fact that Liu Shaoqi died miserably and helplessly at the early stage of the Cultural Revolution. Still, some popular views indicated that several people at ministerial level were Mao Zedong's enemies, because they died miserably and helplessly, too.

These popular and common explanations, though they deemed to be reasonable and understandable, are in fact childish or brainless.

First, at the time when Mao Zedong was alive, no one had any practical ability to shaken and challenge his position to a tiny degree. Second, Mao Zedong had indeed many options to defeat his single-person enemy such as Liu Shaoqi or a small group of enemies composed of several persons. Actually

Mao Zedong absolutely had no need to launch the Cultural Revolution to defeat Liu Shaoqi.

Let us first review a piece of Chinese history to demonstrate the possible disaster and danger to launch the Cultural Revolution to defeat Liu Shaoqi. Anyone, who has read the classical Chinese novel, Three Kingdoms or Romance of Three Kingdoms, would recall what was written at the end of chapter two and the beginning of chapter three, which reads [6]:

> "What about it?" said Yuan Shao on meeting him (He Jin).
>
> "She (Empress) will not consent. What can be done?" (said He Jin).
>
> "Call up an army and slay them (ten regular attendants). It is imperative. Never mind her consent!"
>
> "That is an excellent plan," said He Jin. And he sent orders all round to march soldiers to the capital.
>
> But Secretary Chen Lin objected, "Nay! Do not act without due consideration. The proverb says 'To cover the eyes and snatch at swallows is to fool oneself.' If in so small a matter you cannot attain your wish, what of great affairs? Now by virtue of the emperor and with the army under your hand, you are like prancing tiger and soaring dragon: You may do as you please. To use such enormous powers against the eunuchs would bring victory as easily as lighting up a furnace to burn a hair. You only need to act promptly: Use your powers and smite at once, and all the empire will be with you. But to summon forces to the capital, to gather many bold warlords into one spot, each with different schemes, is to turn our weapons against our own person, to place ourselves in the power of another. Nothing but failure can come of it, and havoc will ensue."
>
> "The view of a mere book-worm," said He Jin with a smile.
>
> Then one of those about He Jin suddenly clapped his hands, laughing, "Solving this issue is as easy as turning over one's hand! Why so much talk?"
>
> The speaker was Cao Cao.
>
> What Cao Cao said was this: "The eunuch evil is of very old standing, but the real cause of the present trouble is in the improper influence allowed them by the emperors and the misplaced favoritism they have enjoyed. But a gaoler would be ample force to employ against this kind of evil, and getting rid of the main culprits is quite enough. Why increase confusion by summoning troops from the regions? Any desire to slay all of them will speedily become known, and the plan will fail."

No one can deny the fact that Mao Zedong was extremely knowledgeable in Chinese history, and his wide wisdom. We simply ask: (i) Why should Mao Zedong need to risk the danger to lead an entire country into chaos in order to eliminate a single-person enemy as Liu Shaoqi by launching of Cultural

Revolution? (ii) Why should Mao Zedong need to risk the new power struggle in order to eliminate a single-person enemy as Liu Shaoqi by launching of Cultural Revolution?

Clearly, to initiate a nationwide revolution to eliminate a single-person enemy not only was illogic and danger but also was very stupid and childish. Mao Zedong, who had experienced so many power struggles within the Chinese Communist Party during his lifetime, should clearly not do anything in such a stupid manner. On the other hand, the contemporary Chinese history has already shown how easily to arrest Gang of Four, can we assume that Mao Zedong was less wise than the people who ordered to arrest Gang of Four?

Now, let us see how Mao Zedong could deal with a single-person enemy if Liu Shaoqi was such an enemy. According to Mao Zedong's traditional and personal style, he could quietly wait for the time when Liu Shaoqi would make a mistake, and then easily eliminate him out from the power center. That would be very easy because no one really knew how to build a new China at that moment for the reason that we discussed in the previous chapter.

The contemporary Chinese history shows that Mao Zedong always patiently waited for his enemies to make mistakes during his lifelong revolution, for example, Mao Zedong waited very patiently for Wang Ming to make disastrous mistakes during Chinese civil war. Similarly it would not take many years and long for Liu Shaoqi to make a fatal mistake to easily end his political career.

Mao Zedong's second option if he would have had a single-person enemy. He would call a meeting of the central committee of Chinese Communist Party rather than a politburo meeting. With Mao Zedong's personal reputation, he could easily defeat Li Shaoqi or at worst reconcile or consolidate with him, which would result in the strengthening of Mao Zedong's power. By contrast, Li Shaoqi could do his best to avoid such an open showdown with Mao Zedong at central committee level, because Mao Zedong was far much popular for ordinary party members, and more importantly the ordinary party members were generally not aware of the direct conflict between Mao Zedong and Liu Shaoqi. Still, the Chinese army was a strong support for Mao Zedong rather than for Liu Shaoqi.

Of course, Mao Zedong still had other options, which will be discussed in the following sections. All in all, the most important point in this section is that Mao Zedong had no need to launch a full-scale Cultural Revolution to eliminate a single-person enemy as Liu Shaoqi, or a small group of enemies at ministerial level.

Thus, our above discussion would answer the question of why Mao Zedong could not patiently wait for the time to come when Liu Shaoqi would make fatal mistakes, and the question of why Mao Zedong did not use his popularity in ordinary Chinese Communist Party members to defeat Liu Shaoqi.

The only valid conclusion is that Mao Zedong was unlikely to have a single-person enemy or a small group of enemies, then who was Mao Zedong's enemy, who led Mao Zedong to launch the Cultural Revolution to settle and seal their disputes forever?

Very likely, Mao Zedong was extremely very much unhappy with the entire generation of career bureaucrats, we deduce this theme because the real and true result of the Cultural Revolution is to wipe out the entire generation of career bureaucrats rather than a single Liu Shaoqi or several high ranked officials. Many popular stories about the local and low ranked officials' sufferings during the Cultural Revolution can support this argument.

Mao Zedong should be unhappy with the entire generation of career bureaucrats because it is very easy for anyone to put the blame on her/his subordinates when what she/he planned could not be finished. In this sense, Mao Zedong should be very unhappy with the entire generation of career bureaucrats because of the failures in Great Leap Forward (1958-1961).

Hence, we would arguably suggest that Mao Zedong's enemy before the Cultural Revolution was the entire generation of career bureaucrats, in other words, almost all the officials (cadres) in all Chinese administrative systems from the very top to the lowest level.

Perhaps, Mao Zedong could feel unhappy with all the young generation educated by Chinese educational system, and he could feel them useless for the future after the Cultural Revolution. Otherwise, Mao Zedong would not treat the Chinese educational system so badly. Actually two types of people, career bureaucrats and intellectuals, were treated very badly during the Cultural Revolution. Based on different treatments, they should be Mao Zedong's enemies.

3.2. MAO ZEDONG'S OPTIONS

After defined the Mao Zedong's enemy, we could try to think the options, which Mao Zedong could use to deal with his enemies. Now let us list them one by one and consider their possibility and suitability.

Perhaps, the easiest way to deal with a single-person enemy is the assassination as history frequently shows. Naturally, Mao Zedong could use this approach to silence Liu Shaoqi if Liu Shaoqi would be Mao Zedong's single-person enemy. We could believe that this approach was possible because Mao Zedong still had the control on the Chinese army and security system. However, Mao Zedong did not apply this approach.

We may have several explanations for not adopting of this approach: (i) it would not be the Mao Zedong's style as we analyzed that Mao Zedong liked to wait patiently for his enemy's the fatal mistakes; (ii) Mao Zedong lost his control on the Chinese army and security system; and (iii) Liu Shaoqi had an exceptional ability to avoid such assassination, which could be possible because Liu Shaoqi had multi-year experience to work in the areas under the Kuomintang (Nationalist Party) control.

Actually, the plan of assassination was not unimaginable because Lin Biao planned to assassinate Mao Zedong, while some accounts suggested that Lin Biao was actually assassinated by Mao Zedong's order.

At any rate, the assassination did not occur in this aspect, which could support our analysis that Mao Zedong did not launch the Cultural Revolution only for the sake of Liu Shaoqi, or Liu Shaoqi would not be the only Mao Zedong's enemy.

Another option, which could be put on the table, would be the coup d'etat using small numbers of Chinese army. Actually, this would be very easy to be done if the accounts on the arresting of Gang of Four are true. According to these accounts, the arresting of Gang of Four appeared to be quite easy with dozens of soldiers. It appeared that any member of Gang of Four did not have any bodyguards within Zhongnanhai, which more importantly implicated that the Zhongnanhai could function as any resident courtyard in China. So Mao Zedong could invite his enemies to visit him and arrest them at his home. However, Mao Zedong did not choose this option, for which there could be several reasons: (i) the coup d'etat is suitable to deal with a small number, but concentrated enemies, so the natural conclusion would be that Mao Zedong had too many enemies to apply the coup d'etat to deal with them; (ii) Mao Zedong lost his control on the Chinese army, so he could not use them to make the coup d'etat, however this was unlikely because Mao Zedong created the Chinese army and never lost his control and influence on the Chinese army; (iii) the Beijing garrison could overpower the elite army, which would try to conduct the coup d'etat, this could be possible because Beijing city government strictly controlled Beijing as evidenced by the fact that Mao

Zedong could not publish his article to launch the Cultural Revolution in Beijing's newspapers, but in Shanghai's newspapers as one account said.

Of course, the above-mentioned options were all in a clandestine manner, which could arouse suspicious in Mao Zedong's enemies. Nevertheless, Mao Zedong could use the clandestine approach to defeat his enemy, if they were numbered, for example, one or two persons. It could be easily done.

However, Mao Zedong did not use these options at all. Therefore the possible explanations would be: (i) Mao Zedong could have too many enemies, thus the murdering of one or two could not be significant enough to change the course, (ii) Mao Zedong could be closely monitored by his enemies, therefore Mao Zedong could not have a tiny possibility to do so, and (iii) Mao Zedong did not trust anyone anymore.

We also need to consider whether Mao Zedong had open options if we defined the above options as clandestine options.

The first open option would be to wage a war, for example, to attack the Taiwan. In fact there were sufficient reasons to attack Taiwan, which would also be easy to obtain the support from all Chinese people, because people living in that time still hated very much the Kuomintang (Nationalist Party). During an open and intensive war, Mao Zedong's enemies could either die in the fighting or dismiss due to failure. Actually China just finished a small-scale war with India in 1962.

The reasons that Mao Zedong did not use this open option to wage a war could be that: (i) such a war could not eliminate Mao Zedong's enemies although each large-scale war in human history can bring a new generation of people into power, and put the old generation out of power; (ii) the Chinese army did not have the ability to cross the Taiwan strait; and (iii) the war with Taiwan could be very much costly in consideration of the cost of Korean War, Hence, perhaps the war, which could not eliminate Mao Zedong's enemies, would be the main reason.

At this point, although we cannot say that we have exhausted our options, to the best of my knowledge, I cannot think out any other options to eliminate Mao Zedong's enemies.

Naturally, we must be amazed by the Mao Zedong's option, the Cultural Revolution, which was indeed the great invention in human history. Actually the Cultural Revolution as an option is far out of our visions, but Mao Zedong thought of it. Actually, the Cultural Revolution was the option many Chinese people experienced and discussed afterwards.

Of course, we still have the final option, which could be no action or option, that is, Mao Zedong would do nothing but would stay at his position as

Marshal Zhu De did. In this case, we could assume that Mao Zedong would certainly have a quiet and luxury life, which Liu Shaoqi and others would not do anything to endanger or change, because this type of life would not affect Liu Shaoqi's plan and his interests.

3.3. MAO ZEDONG'S AIMS

Our analyses in previous sections clearly indicates that Mao Zedong did not need to launch a Cultural Revolution to defeat a single-person enemy or a small group of enemies, and we also discussed all the options, which we can think out for Mao Zedong to defeat his enemies. However, Mao Zedong used his own invented option, the Cultural Revolution. Thus, arguably the aim of Cultural Revolution could not be a power struggle between Mao Zedong and his potential and natural enemies, but could be the struggle between two lines inside the Chinese Communist Party as Mao Zedong always stated. However, even the Cultural Revolution could be the struggle between two lines inside the Chinese Communist Party, it is highly likely that we deeply underestimated Mao Zedong's ambition if we look back the final results of Cultural Revolution.

Although there are many accounts to explain of why Mao Zedong initiated the Cultural Revolution, these reasons were more likely to favor the thoughts produced by ordinary people, who are really very far away either from Mao Zedong or from the power center, needless to mention that they are far, far away from Mao Zedong's mental activities. More importantly, the accounts came from the people, who have no state duties, thus they are accustomed to reason their accounts from their limited experience, mixed with family accounts and love affairs, which are the easiest things to imagine. Of course, I have no experience on state duty too, but I at least know my weakness in this regard and try my best to put all the problems in front of Mao Zedong and try to think out the solutions and compare them with the history.

Still, it is very unfortunate that these popular thoughts focus themselves only on how Mao Zedong could eliminate a single-person enemy, did not consider what to be done after a successful elimination of Liu Shaoqi, if we consider the scale and depth of the Cultural Revolution. Thus, Mao Zedong should have a clear view on what he would do after the Cultural Revolution as he had a clear view on what to do after the World War II and after Chinese civil war (1946-1949).

Still, if Mao Zedong's aim was only limited to eliminate Liu Shaoqi or a group of enemies, he could easily use any option, which we have discussed in the previous section. If we only consider that Mao Zedong has such an aim, we certainly once again deeply underestimate Mao Zedong's ambition. In fact, even the aim to win the struggle between two lines inside Chinese Communist Party appears too small for Mao Zedong's ambition. All Mao Zedong's poems and work clearly demonstrated his great ambitions.

Therefore, Mao Zedong's aim to launch the Cultural Revolution was clear beyond the timescale of Cultural Revolution, that is, Mao Zedong should spend a lot of time to consider what to do after the Cultural Revolution.

An important fact, which draws my special attention, is that Mao Zedong lost his enormous power either step-by-step or suddenly at least two to three years ahead of the launching the Cultural Revolution. The question raised here is what Mao Zedong was doing from 1963 to 1966, if he did no have the day-to-day administrative job at state level. This means that Mao Zedong would have at least two or three years to consider (i) his options on how to restore his power or how to defeat his enemies, and (ii) his prospective and plans in the post-Cultural Revolution ear. For the second consideration, Mao Zedong should also have to consider if his life would be long enough to do what he planned to do in post-Cultural Revolution ear otherwise he should carefully choose a successor.

Considering Mao Zedong's age, he would perhaps well know that he would have not much time left after ending the Cultural Revolution. Mao Zedong should calculate all these three considerations at least to build his aim.

Another way to look at Mao Zedong's aim is to see whether the Cultural Revolution made the Chinese society forward or backward. Evidently, Mao Zedong tried to put Chinese society forward in terms of thoughts and culture because the Cultural Revolution was often marked as destroying the so-called Chinese heritages rather than restoring the so-called Chinese heritages. Of course, this made many intellectuals hate Mao Zedong very much.

Moreover, the human history shows that anyone, who launches a revolution, is not to launch a revolution for the sake of revolution, but for the time after revolution. Therefore, Mao Zedong's aim must direct to the period after the Cultural Revolution.

Arguably, Mao Zedong's final aim would be to solve all the problems during the Cultural Revolution at state level rather than at personal level. This nevertheless is related to Mao Zedong's view on what the communist society would be as Mao Zedong can be fully regarded as an idealist, while Deng Xiaoping can be regarded as a very practical man. However, one thing is certain that Mao Zedong did not spend his youth abroad as many other Chinese leaders in the same generation did, thus Mao Zedong would have less clear and concrete views on what the communist society would be. Another certain fact is that Mao Zedong did not master any foreign languages although it was said that Mao Zedong attempted to learn the German language in order to read the Karl Marx's books in original language rather than translated versions.

On the other hand, Mao Zedong did travel to the USSR in person and his close fellow-comrades would have enough time to tell their experience in foreign countries during their free time, especially during the second Sino-Japanese War.

So we would arguably suggest that Mao Zedong might have an accurate, precise and reliable view on what to do after the Cultural Revolution. This could be one of the reasons of why the Cultural Revolution took so long.

Actually, not only Chinese leaders, nor Soviet leaders, nor the leaders in western world would have an accurate, precise and reliable view on what the communism should be, would be, and looks like.

Therefore, Mao Zedong's aim for launching of the Cultural Revolution could very likely be:

(i)   To eliminate all the obstacles that Mao Zedong felt to prevent him from doing what he planned to do;

(ii) To create a new culture because Mao Zedong completely look down the Chinese culture, which is similar to the Mao Zedong's admired Chinese writer, Lu Xun,

(iii) To make China and Chinese people be prepared for new tasks after the Cultural Revolution.

In principle, the Chinese people like the social stability very much, which is certainly an important Chinese characteristic, and we cannot exclude this characteristic from Mao Zedong. Therefore Mao Zedong should weight the social stability against the social chaos carefully, and try to find a pay-off point between them.

3.4. PREPARATIONS FOR CULTURAL REVOLUTION

Many popular stories describe the occurrence of Cultural Revolution as simple and straightforward as they have a dinner at their home or have a quarrel with his housewife, perhaps this over-simplicity is due to the following facts: (i) Mao Zedong once said that the revolution is not a dinner party, but many people consider the revolution as simple as a dinner party; (ii) more likely many writers mixed too much personal sufferings in their books when considering addressing the issues, which we analyze in this book; (iii) more importantly these writers never consider the issues that I will discuss afterwards.

However, any practical and common sense tell us that Mao Zedong needed to prepare everything for the Cultural Revolution, because Mao Zedong was not an imprudent person at all, so at least Mao Zedong needed to consider, if not be prepared, the following issues for the preparation for the Cultural Revolution. As a state leader, Mao Zedong should certainly consider the worst scenario before launching of the Cultural Revolution.

The first issue for the preparation for the Cultural Revolution was whether the Mainland China had sufficient food to feed the people during the Cultural Revolution, because the reduction of food would be expected when any revolution comes. Meanwhile, China had just experienced the three years of natural disasters from 1958 to 1961 [7], when the food shortage was the biggest problem. Thus, Mao Zedong should at first consider whether the food would be enough for seven hundreds of millions of Chinese people (the estimated population then) for several years even for a decade. Otherwise there would be another famine disaster during Cultural Revolution, when food was running out it could lead to profound and unimaginable effects on Chinese social system because the power structure will be destroyed in planned Cultural Revolution.

The second issue was whether the factories, schools, hospitals and local governments continued to pay their employees salaries. Without salary, these people could not live, but they would be far less productive if they would attend to the Cultural Revolution, so where money would come from to pay them should be a big problem.

The third issue was whether the Chinese government needed the necessary taxation for raising the necessary funds or whether the Chinese government needed to issue government bonds in order to borrow money from the Chinese people for a no-one-work Cultural Revolution. In fact, the Chinese government claimed during the Cultural Revolution that China became the first country in the world without borrowing money either from her people or aboard after paying back some debts to the USSR. This is indeed amazing.

The fourth issue was whether any foreign powers would invade the Mainland China during the Cultural Revolution, because at that time China had few friendly countries surrounded: China had a very bad relationship with USSR, consequently a bad relationship with Mongolia and the relationship with North Korea deteriorated. Besides, the US army was fighting in Vietnam, and China just had a war with India. Mao Zedong should consider the possibility that any armed conflicts could occur during the Cultural Revolution because the foreign powers would certainly watch closely and try to seize an opportunity. From this viewpoint, Mao Zedong could have the plan to launch the Culture Revolution long before the time he did because he might have to wait for the Chinese nuclear bombs, which was succeeded around 1964 otherwise he could have no weapons to defend the Mainland China.

The fifth issue was whether the Kuomintang (Nationalist Party) could invade the Mainland China from Taiwan or plot something during the Cultural Revolution because any revolution would easily lead many unhappy and unsatisfied people, who would be subject to Kuomintang's influence.

The sixth issue was how the Chinese administrative systems would function during the Cultural Revolution because one of the aims of Cultural Revolution was to wipe out the whole generation of career bureaucrats in all the administrative systems. This was also particularly important, that is to say, who would run day-to-day administrative jobs during the Cultural Revolution.

The seventh issue was whether Mao Zedong could keep China from inflation, which would be a natural result of dysfunction of economy during the Cultural Revolution.

So, we can see the preparation for the Cultural Revolution is not as simple and straightforward as many people considered. Mao Zedong needed to prepare everything from logistic, international political, internal political, and so on and so forth, almost everything needed to be considered.

Perhaps, Mao Zedong personally did not consider that the Cultural Revolution would take as long as ten years. This argument is deduced from the fact that the Chinese economy almost collapsed before the ending of Cultural Revolution as said after the Cultural Revolution. This would suggest that the economic preparation for the Cultural Revolution was not sufficient enough for ten years.

3.5. MAO ZEDONG'S FORCES AND REWARDS

If Mao Zedong's enemy was not limited to Liu Shaoqi, but the entire generation of career bureaucrats, then Mao Zedong did need to mobilize millions of people to defeat these powerful enemies at different locations and at different steps of career ladders.

A question, any leader as Mao Zedong should carefully consider before such a massively popular political movement, was how to reward these millions of people, who will destroy the entire generation of career bureaucrats. Someone might wonder whether Mao Zedong needed to consider this issue, even never considers this issue. Let us once again review what was written in classical Chinese novel, Three Kingdoms or Romance of Three Kingdoms, because this novel really reveals what happened at kingdom level rather than at personal or family level with endless love affairs [8]:

> Having conquered Hanzhong, Liu Bei sent Liu Feng, Meng Da, and Wang Ping to take Shangyong. The Commander of the city, Shen Dan, and his colleagues, knowing that Cao Cao had retreated, offered their submission. After confidence had been restored among the people, Liu Bei rewarded his army generously, and they were all joyful.
>
> It was after this that the general body of the officials decided to urge Liu Bei to assume the title of 'Emperor', but they dared not tell him so. However, they sent up a petition to Zhuge Liang.
>
> He replied, 'I have already decided on this course.'
>
> So Zhuge Liang and Fa Zheng headed a deputation that went in to see their lord.
>
> They said, 'Now that Cao Cao really holds the reins of authority, the people are without a true sovereign. Our lord, your kindness and sense of justice have spread throughout the empire. You have restored peace over the two River Lands, and your becoming an emperor would be according to God's will and the desire of the people. Then by right and title you could destroy rebels. This matter should not be delayed, and we pray you choose the auspicious day.'
>
> But Liu Bei evinced great surprise, and replied, 'Your words, O Instructor, are wrong. Although I am of the imperial house, yet I am but a minister. And to do this thing would be rebellion against Han.
>
> Zhuge Liang replied, 'Not so. Today the empire is riven, and many of the bolder spirits have seized upon and claim the rule of various portions. The talented of the empire and the virtuous among officials, who have risked death and lost their lives in serving those above them, all desire to have the opportunity of serving a true emperor and doing service for a true Throne.[1]

---

[1] Author's note: here, the translation was wrong, it should be translated as follows: all desire to have the opportunity of becoming famous and being rewarded.

Now, if you insist on modestly maintaining your righteous way, I fear that you will lose popular support. My lord, I wish that you should reflect upon this.'

Naturally Mao Zedong should consider how to reward the people, who would help him to defeat his enemies. When now, after ending of the Cultural Revolution for so many years, we look back this issue, we should be amazed by Mao Zedong's consideration.

Mao Zedong extremely clever decided to use the youths; the majority of them were middle school students, these students in fact were less than 18 years old ranged from 13 to 18 years of age and could not be classified as adult by any criteria. Thus, these youths do not need the rewards such as titles, positions, money, house, etc. The young students were too honest to require any rewards, because they were idealists, who did not need any rewards, even they would look down any rewards. Besides, the young students were well below the age of marriage, so they had no children to take care of, and they had no family to be worried, they had no social experience, they virtually had no personal belongings to be afraid of losing. Moreover, they had no personal ambitions on money, but a plenty of time.

In addition, the mobilization of young students would not have too much negative impact on the Chinese economy, simply because young students did not work either in farms or in factories. As Mao Zedong already looked down the Chinese educational system, so the issue that the young student would learn much less during the Cultural Revolution would become less concerned.

Taking all these considerations into account, the young students should naturally become the best candidates and should be the major force for planned extremely large-scale revolution.

Another important force, which should fall into Mao Zedong's mind, would be the working class, i.e. the workers in factories in China. Personally, Mao Zedong did not have too many contacts with purely working class although Mao Zedong had been the mine An Yuan for a while, but certainly the working class was not a type of people whom Mao Zedong was extremely familiar with. Actually, Mao Zedong was very familiar with students, not only because Mao Zedong's early revolution career was more or less related to students' political movements, but also because the Chinese revolution attracted many students, especially during the second Sino-Japanese War. Of course, Mao Zedong was also very familiar with peasants, not only because Mao Zedong grew up in countryside, but also the Chinese revolution was mainly conducted in countryside. Of course, Mao Zedong was also very familiar with soldiers because Mao Zedong's career was always related to the Chinese army.

Although the classical Marx's theory indicates that the working class is the main force in revolution, Mao Zedong in fact did not plan to massively mobilize the working class in the Cultural Revolution. Perhaps, he would not again risk the Chinese economy, but more probably Mao Zedong did not have much confidence on this force because Mao Zedong was a very prudent person. Therefore, Mao Zedong was highly likely to consider the use of the working class in somewhat later stage of Cultural Revolution. On the other hand, the working class did not need to be rewarded too much, because they had their career ladder in their own factory. Practically, any estimation would suggest that the number of likely-to-be-mobilized workers were far below the number of likely-to-be-mobilized young students.

The third force would be millions of Chinese peasants, whom Mao Zedong was extremely well familiar with. However, Mao Zedong cleverly did not use this force, because (i) the Cultural Revolution would be mainly conducted in urban areas rather than in rural areas, (ii) Mao Zedong might not like the idea to call millions of peasants into cities, which would lead the conflict between working class and peasant class, and big logistic problems, (iii) Mao Zedong could be disappointed by Chinese peasants because his reform in countryside did not increase much productions, (iv) Mao Zedong perhaps mainly hoped to maintain the Chinese agricultural productions during the Cultural Revolution, and (v) Mao Zedong certainly knew that the rewards for peasants would be their residence in cities when they would come into cities, which was impossible.

The fourth force, whom Mao Zedong was most familiar with and had a great confidence on, was the Chinese army. But Mao Zedong should consider the danger of invasion from every direction, so Mao Zedong would not use this force until the last minute. On the other hand, the Chinese army was generally not familiar with the structure of Chinese career bureaucrats, so it would be somewhat difficult to operate in civil affairs. Of course, the young students were not familiar with this structure too. The Chinese history clearly shows that traditionally the civil servants rather than the army operated China in most of historical times. This perhaps would be a reason of why Mao Zedong did not use the Chinese army at the first stage of the Cultural Revolution. The rewards for Chinese army would be much complicated, Mao Zedong's way was to put these army officers into civil positions charging some duties as he did after the creation of People's Republic of China. If the entire career bureaucrats would be destroyed during the planned Cultural

Revolution, then Mao Zedong could simply reward the army officers the empty civil positions as rewards.

We can see the forces, Mao Zedong would use, and the way, Mao Zedong would reward, are very much economic. This is indeed an economic way to conduct a revolution.

On the one hand, the choice of forces fully suggests Mao Zedong's cleverness, but on the other hand, this could also suggest that Mao Zedong's enemies were extremely strong so Mao Zedong had to rely on students rather than central committee of Chinese Communist Party.

Chapter 4

COUNTER-MEASURES

Political calculation, yes. Political feelings, no.

— Tony Blair, A Journey: My Political Life [9]

The main forces, which Mao Zedong used at the earlier stage of the Cultural Revolution, were the Red Guards. These terrible Red Guards in fact were composed of millions of students from middle school aged from 13 to 18 years old. Technically, they were not adults according to any constitution in anywhere in the world: they were not entitled to express their political view, they could be classified as teenagers, and even they could be regarded as child soldiers without real weapons.

If we consider the above facts, we would feel amazed and stunned that millions of career bureaucrats, some of whom experienced two Chinese civil wars, Sino-Japanese War and Korean War, could so easily be defeated by teenagers. Some of these career bureaucrats were once true fighters and warriors, but submitted and subdued their fate to the mentally and physically immature Red Guards.

Is it a sign of how fragile and weak the Chinese career bureaucratic system was? If it would be so, then Mao Zedong was very well aware of the weakness of Chinese career bureaucratic system, so he could use the Red Guards to destroy this system.

Is it an ironic laughter for these revolutionary fighters and warriors? Why could these career bureaucrats not organize some counter-measures against Mao Zedong's Cultural Revolution to save them from such a brutal fate?

Also it would be very surprising that so many powerfully revolutionary cadres readily and easily handed out their power, and surrounded their fate to the Red Guards, and did not know what to do to change their ill fate.

The question now raised is whether Liu Shaoqi and his associates could take their counter-measures against Mao Zedong and his Cultural Revolution if they knew their final fates at the beginning of the Cultural Revolution. This possibility could not be excluded not only because Mao Zedong once said that any reactivates would not voluntarily withdraw from historical stage, but more important was that these people still had very important powers in their hands at the beginning of the Cultural Revolution.

So the counter-measures mean the conflicts between Mao Zedong and the people whose fate were certainly doomed. However, we did not see any organized counter-measures have been taken place during the Cultural Revolution besides Lin Biao's plan to make a coup d'etat, which eventually failed.

It looks like that Mao Zedong had so many ways and options to fight his enemy at different areas, while his enemy could fight him in only limited ways with very limited options. Actually these enemies could only submit their fate to Mao Zedong, and wait for their fall.

4.1. POSSIBLE COUNTER-MEASURES

Naturally, the counter-measures could be taken place at any level of Chinese administrative system, and even all the ordinary Chinese people. Let us first review what was written about the retreat of Alexander the Great from his adventure to conquer India [10]:

> "Alexander was greatly troubled and distressed. A disaffection in a small part of an army may be put down by decisive measures; but when the determination to resist is universal, it is useless for any commander, however imperious and absolute in temper, to attempt to withstand it."

So, if all the Chinese people from very top brass to the lowest grassroots would have gone against Mao Zedong's decision of launching of the Cultural Revolution, the Cultural Revolution would have been stopped, as we have witnessed that the passive resistance that finally stopped Mao Zedong's "Down to the Countryside Movement", which sent the millions of Red Guards to remotely rural areas in China (also see Section 5.1, Chapter 5). In our

Chinese proverb, we would say: bu liao liao zhi, in Chinese pronunciation, an action/movement ends without order to end.

However, we have not seen the occurrence of this type of massive resistance in the eve of launching of the Cultural Revolution, nor during the Cultural Revolution, either at Chinese Communist Party level or at ordinary Chinese people level. So we have to conclude that the Chinese people from top to bottom had no such a will, so the nationwide large-scale counter-measure could not be possible. Although many popular writers indicated how ordinary Chinese people and they hated the Cultural Revolution, these hatreds rose after the Cultural Revolution at the best because we have not seen any organized counter-measures from the ordinary Chinese people.

If the ordinary Chinese people had no intention and no way to take any counter-measures, then Liu Shaoqi and his associates could open a meeting at the level of central committee of Chinese Communist Party to prevent the Cultural Revolution from launching, because they still controlled many places, for example, the Beijing city government successfully prevented the Mao Zedong's from publishing something in the newspapers run in Beijing, which led to Mao Zedong to publish it in Shanghai.

If there was no way to prevent Mao Zedong from launching of the Cultural Revolution, then we should ask whether there would be the way to prevent the Red Guards from damaging and destroying China. This was so because it was still quite puzzling and bizarre that the powerful adults could not defend themselves against the teenagers, Red Guards. If the Chinese people could take some counter-measures against the Red Guards, then the Cultural Revolution would not be so brutal. Let us consider several options:

(i) Could it be possible for a part of members of Communist Party to submit an appeal to Mao Zedong to declare the Red Guards illegal regarding their age because Mao Zedong supported these teenagers? But the history did not show any such a sign, so the explanations could be that either a majority of party members considered the appeal unnecessary or no one dared do so. However, it was more likely that the Chinese people had no concept that teenagers have no legal right in politics.

(ii) Considering the number of Red Guards, the number of people taking counter-measures could be somewhat equal if the counter-measure party did not take weapons. In such case, any fraction of Chinese professional classes did not have such a big number of people besides peasants in countryside. Also it would be very difficult to mobilize such sizable peasants against the Red Guards.

(iii) Could it be possible that the Chinese parents did something to prevent their children from becoming the Red Guards? Perhaps, there were some individual cases, where the parents played a role to prevent their Red Guards children from madness. However, the joining of Red Guards was a glory during the Cultural Revolution. How could individual parent take any counter-measure against their children?

(iv) Could the Chinese educational system play some counter-measure role? Impossible, because the first target of Red Guards aimed at schoolteachers. Perhaps, this was Mao Zedong's plan because it needed to defeat schoolteachers in order that Red Guards could go to streets to destroy a whole generation of career bureaucrats.

(v) So the only efficient and effective counter-measure against Red Guards was to use the armed Chinese army. In fact, there were several cases during the early stage of the Cultural Revolution that the Mao Zedong approved the Chinese army to defeat Red Guards when Red Guards threatened the central government. And in Section 12.4, Chapter 12, we arguably suggested that Deng Xiaoping learned this lesson and applied it.

(vi) Another counter-measure was to disband the Red Guards, which happened after the Cultural Revolution in a quite and unnoticeable manner. Perhaps, Deng Xiaoping initiated this idea to disband the Red Guards. However, the brutal role of Red Guards was partially minimized during the Cultural Revolution, when Mao Zedong used the slogan that the working class to lead everything to partially control the Red Guards.

(vii) Of course, it could be possible to use the marshal law to disband the Red Guards. Perhaps, Deng Xiaoping learned this lesson and applied it (also see Section 12.4, Chapter 12).

So far, the counter-measures, which we considered, were related to the measures against the launching of the Cultural Revolution and measures against the lawless Red Guards. All these measures should be efficient and effective at large-scale.

There were still options in hands, for example, to create another central committee of Chinese Communist Party, as Zhang Guotao did during the Long March. However, it would be very difficult because no place in China could be suitable to create another central committee of Chinese Communist Party. This was so, because the creation of another central committee of Communist Party in China would mean the beginning of civil war. However, the pre-condition for a civil war would be the existence of warlords. As we discussed in Section 2.2, Chapter 2, Mao Zedong had effectively and efficiently eliminate such a possibility immediately after the creation of People's Republic of China. Even, there were some warlords who had such a plan, an important question would be whether these warlords could get the economic and weapon support from foreign countries because this was the way that all the previous Chinese warlords lived and did. More important would be whether this newly created central committee of Chinese Communist Party could be widely recognized.

Now we consider whether there were options that one could use against his/her ill fate. These were certainly small-scale counter-measures. Actually, we need to know the options in the people whose fate was definitely gloomy.

Still, we ask whether the career bureaucrats could take some counter-measures against their ill fate and whether there were such options? For example, could they ask the fair trials rather than be tortured to death? Although 'Mao Zedong did not deliberately destroy the law enforcement system during the early stage of the Cultural Revolution, this option was still unlikely. This was so because the Chinese law enforcement system was never perfectly and fully developed, generally under-developed, so not only the ordinary Chinese people but also the career bureaucrats had no concept to look for the justice from the Chinese law enforcement system.

The most notable case that people took counter-measures would be the Lin Biao's case, which provided a strong example of counter-measures, by which Lin Biao planned to assassinate Mao Zedong.

4.2. POSSIBLE REASONS FOR NO COUNTER-MEASURES

As we have seen that there were almost no known counter-measures, which uncountable career bureaucrats could take before and during the Cultural Revolution, so the natural question would be why they did not take counter-measures against the Cultural Revolution and against the Red Guards?

Could we say that these uncountable career bureaucrats lacked political calculations as well as political feelings? Could no parties were formed against the Cultural Revolution and against the Red Guards? Could no officials of government begin to conceive of a plan of escaping their ill fate? Really, nothing could be done but wait in dismay and fear for the sure and inevitable doom?

Actually, a very small-scale counter-measure could be easily taken under the name to defend the Cultural Revolution and to be loyal to Mao Zedong, because there were uncountable factions during the earlier stage of the Cultural Revolution that no one knew and understood which faction was revolutionary. This counter-measure at least and at worst could defend a local career bureaucrat against personal torture.

Perhaps, an important implication that Mao Zedong's enemies did not take any counter-measures was that they did not consider themselves to be Mao Zedong's enemies. Or Mao Zedong's enemies did not consider themselves to be the target of the Cultural Revolution.

If this would be true, then all the statements that Mao Zedong launched the Cultural Revolution for the sake to eliminate Liu Shaoqi and his associates would not be valid and melt down, because Liu Shaoqi and his associates did not take any currently-known counter-measures.

Another possible reason that no major counter-measures were taken could be that every career bureaucrat agreed with the necessity of the Cultural Revolution. If this would be so, then it looked like what Mao Zedong planned to do was quite right.

Perhaps, the most convincing reason was that the Chinese career bureaucrats were accustomed to execute everything ordered from their superiors without future consideration. If this would be so, it would be the tragic fate for the Chinese people and career bureaucrats themselves alike, because those career bureaucrats were living machines to execute orders.

There was still a possibility that every career bureaucrat, or some career bureaucrats, considered that the Cultural Revolution was the way to eliminate their own personally hated career bureaucrats, the way to get into a fast track along career ladder, and the way to capitalize them. In such a case, why did they need to take a counter-measure? Potentially, they could hope and dream that the longer and the crueler the better the Cultural Revolution was, so they could have sufficient time to defeat their personal enemy and could go fast along the career ladder.

On the other hand, the incapability to defend their interests and fate when the Cultural Revolution came to destroy these officials was also very suggestive. This implies that the majority of the ordinary Chinese people did not like these career bureaucrats at the best, but did hate them at the worst. This furthermore suggests that the administrative officials in China were a class far away from getting the ordinary Chinese people's support. Thus, they might have planned some counter-measures in some ways but they could not implement their plans into actions without the support from ordinary Chinese people.

In fact, many administrative officials indeed suffered a lot during the Cultural Revolution, so we have many stories on personal suffering during the Cultural Revolution related to these administrative officials. These stories could ironically support the above argument.

Perhaps, many ordinary Chinese people had a feeling that they needed to conduct some type of revolution in order to change something they did not like. This argument is very convincing, anyone, who has his/her own working experience in China rather than went abroad immediately after finishing university education, would say that the low ranked officials in China are most hateful, because they are rude and press the ordinary people to a degree that they cannot live peacefully.

Another possibility could be that the extremely chaotic situation would lead the career bureaucrats to have no way to organize an effective defense. Or, a totally chaotic situation prevented Mao Zedong's enemies to plan any effective counter-measures against Mao Zedong and his Red Guards.

All in all, there could be many reasons of why the Chinese career bureaucrats did not take actions against the Cultural Revolution and Red Guards, which leaves the room for exploring it in the future.

Chapter 5

DAMAGE CONTROL DURING CULTURAL REVOLUTION

To make the best of bad business and go back pleasantly and like men.

— *Mary Mapes Dodge, Hans Brinker or The Silver Skates [11]*

For many people, who underwent the Cultural Revolution, the Cultural Revolution was indeed the darkest chapter in their living memory, a nightmare, which no one could dream it out previously. Of course, our current knowledge does not provide the evidence on whether the designers of Cultural Revolution had predicted such a profound result, such a nightmare.

As we discussed in Chapter 3, Mao Zedong had the full- and deep-designed preparations for the Cultural Revolution, therefore Mao Zedong should certainly consider some measures for damage control in order that he could accomplish his plan without losing his power at personal level but he could change the country at national level.

In this Chapter, we would try to examine whether Mao Zedong had run the damage control actions during the Cultural Revolution, which can also provide us with additional evidence to support and reconfirm our viewpoints that Mao Zedong launched the Cultural Revolution with full preparations, so the Cultural Revolution was not a simple power struggle between Mao Zedong and Liu Shaoqi.

Also, these analyses can let us know how Mao Zedong stabilized the chaotic situations in China during the first period of Cultural Revolution.

In general, the damage control is not an easy job simply because no one can turn the clock back to let the bad situation return back to its original state. Therefore, the real damage control is not only very challenging but also requires new ideas and thoughts simply because no one can turn back the clock. Still, one should consider what would happen if there were no damage controls.

Certainly, the biggest damage control was to prevent the Cultural Revolution from becoming a bloody history with bloodbath. From this view, the damage control was very well done because the China did not fall into a civil war with armed conflicts. The option Mao Zedong adopted was to prevent the Chinese army totally from being involved in the Cultural Revolution.

By clear contrast to the fact that few counter-measures were taken before and during the Cultural Revolution, many damage control measures were taken during the Cultural Revolution, though which we could learn a little bit so-called leadership art, however we would focus our efforts in analysis on only several aspects. Arguably the activities in Chinese society step by step came back to normal with these damage control measures.

The real history shows that Mao Zedong generally ran several damage controls simultaneously rather than ran a single damage control to a single case. However, we have to analyze the damage control one by one.

5.1. RED GUARDS

When looking back history, we could say the second biggest damage control, which Mao Zedong did during the Cultural Revolution, was to find the destination for millions of Red Guards.

Theoretically, it is extremely difficult to control these millions of Red Guards, who went out from their classroom and created a very much chaotic situation in China. The characteristics of these teenagers and youngsters had become violent, brutal and lawless during the Cultural Revolution. However, they were very much loyal to Mao Zedong, especially, after Mao Zedong had reviewed millions of Red Guards in Tiananmen Square at the early stage of Cultural Revolution.

In China, perhaps, only Mao Zedong himself could control and manage these restless and reckless teenagers. These millions of teenagers destroyed almost all the administrative system in China, wiped out the entire generation of career bureaucrats, overthrew almost the whole local authorities and deeply damaged the Chinese cultural heritages. Their impacts were huge and enormous in every aspect of Chinese daily-life in Mainland China. Thus we could generally say that the Red Guards achieved the goals, which Mao Zedong designed before launching of the Cultural Revolution. Even, we could arguably say that the Red Guards reached the goals, which were far more beyond Mao Zedong's designed plan.

After the storm of Red Guards, Mao Zedong could find that he practically and actually opened the Pandora's box. Every damage cannot be undone although Mao Zedong might not want to undo because the Red Guards played the decisive role to lead the Cultural Revolution to reach the Mao Zedong's goals. Without Red Guards, the Cultural Revolution could certainly not be so intensive.

As we analyzed in Section 3.5, Chapter 3, these Red Guards did not need any rewards, they needed to continue their revolution in everywhere inside China, even in the world if they could go abroad.

Meanwhile, these Red Guards had grown up during the early stage of the Cultural Revolution, so it was definitely impossible to send them back to their abandoned classrooms again. Besides, millions of new babies had born during that period of time. More importantly, nothing could restrict the mind of millions of young men and women in their small and dull classrooms again. In fact, there were no places for them in school because the new children and tanagers needed these places, too.

Although the Red Guards created so many damages in China, no one can deny the very basic fact that the Red Guards were uncorrupted, naive, innocent and high in their moral standards in general because they were boys and girls when they did their damage to the Chinese society.

Therefore, the damage control, next to preventing the Cultural Revolution from falling into a bloodbath civil war, was to control the restless and reckless Red Guards, who still had a full passion for revolution. This was so because the first stage of the Cultural Revolution had already reached the goal. The Red Guards themselves had already become a national problem although they did not act for personal gains to any tiny degree.

Mao Zedong could consider the options to send these millions of Red Guards to Chinese factories, because anyway these factories were running the planned economic model without problems to absorb these youngsters. Perhaps, Mao Zedong considered that these Red Guards could not be satisfied with routine factory work in dark workshops, so Mao Zedong did not adopt the option to send the Red Guards into factories.

Mao Zedong also did not accept the option to send the Red Guards into the Chinese army although that would be the really greatest dream for most of Red Guards. Perhaps, Mao Zedong would like to see a disciplined Chinese army without the disturbing of Red Guards. Practically, Mao Zedong should know that the Chinese army could not absorb so many youngsters, especially there were an equal amount of young women in Red Guards, and no army in the world could absorb so many female soldiers.

On the other hand, Mao Zedong clearly knew that these Red Guards knew nothing besides following Mao Zedong's instructions closely and executing Mao Zedong's instructions exaggeratedly. This was so because the studies in those young Red Guards were totally abandoned, and they were literally unable to do anything that required special knowledge and technique. This assumption was almost certain because Mao Zedong had the chances to contact with Red Guards during the early stage of the Cultural Revolution and had good conversations with them, from which Mao Zedong could easily make his own judgment. The real fact was that Mao Zedong knew very well that the historical role and mission of Red Guards had overwhelmingly finished.

In short, the Red Guards should be placed in some places to earn their life. Meanwhile, the work should not require special knowledge and technique in order that Red Guards could survive, besides the working places should be isolated to prevent the Red Guards from reassembling together again to make new troubles, and these places should be far away from political center and power center to prevent the Red Guards from continuing new revolution by coming back to the cities again.

Perhaps, these were the real and true reasons that Mao Zedong initiated the "Down to the Countryside Movement" with slogan, up to the mountains and down to the villages.

Perhaps this was the only choice that only Mao Zedong could think out. This was the only efficient and effective way for the damage control on Red Guards, who were the real and true victims of the Cultural Revolution while to some small degree the other victims were the dead and suffered people caused by the Red Guards. The Red Guards with their restless and reckless characteristics but without any special knowledge and technique could be only confined and polished in remote and uncivilized areas.

All in all, the timing for this damage control was well calculated, because the whole China agreed that the terror created by Red Guards should end. Our analysis in this section is totally different from the popular view, which suggests that the sending of Red Guards to countryside was due to the fact that no job was available in cities without any other consideration either from political view or from damage control view.

5.2. RAMBLING CHILDREN

The next damage control could be how to deal with the children, who were in fact students from primary/elementary schools, even from kindergartens. They were too young to become the Red Guards although there was an organization called Little Red Guards to absorb some these children at primary school level. Still, these Little Red Guards were too little to do anything in Chinese society either physically or mentally.

The amount of this group of children could not be underestimated, because in principle the numbers of students in primary schools and kindergartens were larger than the students in middle schools. These children indeed had nothing to do during the early stage of the Cultural Revolution. They simply rambled everywhere to see what happened because the schools were closed, more exactly, in a very long holiday. This was to say that the schools closed most time, but opened occasionally to call students to attend demonstrations, for example, when the armed conflicts occurred between USSR and China, or to attend celebrations, for example, Mao Zedong issued a new instruction.

These rambling children mostly enjoyed their long vacation for several years, which was also the case for me.

However, they did not become the street children because they still had their parents in family and returned home for eating and sleeping. In general, these children played among themselves happily or rambled along the streets to find out anything new to them.

Perhaps, these small children did not draw Mao Zedong's attention at the beginning of the Cultural Revolution due to the completely chaotic situation in China. Perhaps, these children were related to Mao Zedong's unrevealed plan about what he would do after the Cultural Revolution. The damage control in this sense would be related to the future China rather than the China at the time of the Cultural Revolution.

Therefore, the permanent close of primary and middle schools did not seem to be a good solution. The option, which Mao Zedong chose, was so-called resuming of lesson to conduct the revolution.

However, Mao Zedong was certainly not happy with what he considered belonged to the old educational system, which should be one of targets defined by Mao Zedong when planning the Cultural Revolution. In fact, Mao Zedong personally looked down teachers as well as intellectuals, and considered them useless and hopeless. Naturally, Mao Zedong would not have a great confidence on these teachers and intellectuals, so Mao Zedong invented so-called worker propaganda team composed of workers from factories, and sent them to the schools. These workers, most of them were old workers had bitter experience before the creation of People's Republic of China, loved Mao Zedong although they were far less educated.

Anyway, this damage control worked, because many millions of rambling children returned to their schools regularly, and had something to study during that transition period, which gave Mao Zedong the time to consider what he needed to do in future.

5.3. ECONOMY

During the Cultural Revolution, the Chinese economy decayed especially at the early stage of the Cultural Revolution. I do not know whether this decay was Mao Zedong's intention, but the economic situation certainly was not a joyful picture, especially after the mobilization of millions of Red Guards traveled around country without payment and many factories literally did not produce anything but involved in the conflict between local factions.

After the Cultural Revolution, a popular say was that the Chinese economy was on the edge of total collapse. As all the Chinese definitions, the collapse of Chinese economy is not clearly and numerically defined, thus no one has a real concept on what the collapse of Chinese economy means. However, it was indeed that the daily life during the Cultural Revolution was not easy, not only because the production reduced sharply but also all the self-employed small businesses were shut down on the account that these self-employed small businesses were capitalism. If the undefined statement that the Chinese economy was on the edge of collapse would be correct, then anyway it did not collapse during the Cultural Revolution.

So, it would be very surprising that Chinese economy did not collapse during the Cultural Revolution not only because the domestic productions reduced sharply but also more importantly the Chinese economy was the socialist economy, i.e. the planned economy. As almost all the local authorities were destroyed and the entire generation of career bureaucrats was out of power, arguably and evidently no one would continue to plan and arrange any productions. Without planning, we should really wonder how the salary could be paid to workers, teachers, medical doctors, officials, army officers, policemen, and all the people living on salary? We should also wonder where the money came from if the government did not print money? It was very unlikely that the Chinese government printed a great amount of money during the Cultural Revolution because there was no record on inflation inside China.

We should be more surprised by the fact that China claimed to be the only country without borrowing money either abroad or from her people in the world during the Cultural Revolution. All these unimaginable things reveal the very truth about planned economy, that is, no one could really plan anything in a planned economy or what the authority planned was a paper work or any plan in a planned economy was a waste of time and energy.

At this point, arguably Mao Zedong knew far better about the Chinese economy than we do, even than anyone else did in his generation including experts in economy. This was so because Mao Zedong knew that he could conduct the Cultural Revolution safely without the risk of collapsing of Chinese economy. Mao Zedong should have the confidence on the Chinese economy because he was well aware of the fact that the hunger peasants overthrew almost all the previous Chinese governments in Chinese history, thus he could not dare let Chinese peasants be hunger again during the Cultural Revolution. This once again shows a counter-example to the popular account that the Cultural Revolution was launched for a very simple reason.

Furthermore, if the collapse of Chinese civil administrative system and wiping of career bureaucrats during the Cultural Revolution did not deal a heavily fatal blow to the planned Chinese economy, then arguably the so-called planned economy could only play a tiny role in the whole Chinese economy. This is to say that the Chinese economy was not fully planned at least, while actually the planned economy already led the catastrophic effects before the Cultural Revolution. I really wonder whether Mao Zedong would like to use the opportunity of Cultural Revolution to show how useless the planned economy was?

The Cultural Revolution also demonstrated that the Chinese economy at that time was a more likely to be in the state of self-sufficiency, i.e. an agriculture based economy. Thus, the fact that Mao Zedong did not plan to initiate the peasants to join the Cultural Revolution seemed to not only keep peasants from going into cities but also keep the Chinese economy running.

Anyway, Mao Zedong was certainly not happy with the decaying economy, which fortunately was mainly related to the life in cities. Thus, we could see several damage controls, perhaps the most notable damage control related to the decaying economy would be the so called seizing of revolution and promoting of production. This literately restored the normal economic activities.

5.4. CHAOTIC SITUATION AND REBUILDING OF LOCAL AUTHORITY

For the most people, the memory on the Cultural Revolution would be a totally chaotic situation. This was indeed true for the first phase of Cultural Revolution. Now we should ask why the Cultural Revolution was so chaotic that any civil authority and any civil administrative systems could not function. Certainly, it was a period of anarchism.

When referring to this chaotic situation, Mao Zedong once said that this chaotic situation troubled enemies but trained the revolutionary people. Perhaps, this was what Mao Zedong really felt and thought during the Cultural Revolution. This is so because the chaotic situation prevented any organized counter-measures against Mao Zedong and his Cultural Revolution. On the other hand, we should admit that the Chinese army was generally in good shape and good order during the Cultural Revolution although there were many small-scale incidences occurred inside the Chinese army. Actually the administrative system in Chinese army was totally intact.

We therefore should look at how the Cultural Revolution was initiated? The Cultural Revolution was not initiated through any civil administrative system from top to bottom, but through Mao Zedong's personal support. Also the initial target of the Cultural Revolution was directed to the administrative system and career bureaucrats. Nevertheless, the striking on this target would lead to a chaotic situation in Chinese society.

As the chaotic situation is so different between Chinese army and Chinese society, we could easily get the conclusion that Mao Zedong deliberately created a chaotic situation in Chinese society, mainly in civil administrative system, in order that his enemies could not organize any effective and efficient counter-measures. In such a totally confused chaotic situation, Mao Zedong had no need to defeat his enemies one by one individually, but defeated almost all of them simultaneously with exception of Deng Xiaoping (see Chapter 13).

After wiping out the whole generation of career bureaucrats from all the local and central administrative systems, clearly the chaotic situation would not benefit to anyone else more. At this point, Mao Zedong's main damage control was (i) to send the Red Guards to the remote countryside, and (ii) to rebuild the local authority called revolutionary committee. Of course, there were still several small-sized damage control, for example, the students, who could travel free of charge across the country, were asked to return to their original schools to conduct the revolution.

The rebuilding of local authority through revolutionary committee was a decisive way, by which China was step-by-step becoming less and less chaotic, meanwhile the positions in revolutionary committee also became a reward for the people who actively took part in the Cultural Revolution along with Mao Zedong's line.

Chapter 6

WHAT DID THE CULTURAL REVOLUTION REALLY DO?

It takes three years to build a ship, it takes three centuries to build a tradition.

— Andrew Cunningham (7 January 1883 – 12 June 1963)

Perhaps, Mao Zedong had the intention to use the Cultural Revolution to change the Chinese people's mind through various approaches used in the Cultural Revolution, and Mao Zedong could also have the intention to create a new Chinese culture and new administrative system to run the country. However the Cultural Revolution was not successful in these two regards.

Currently and historically, no one really knows what a whole picture about the new Chinese culture was in Mao Zedong's mind because Mao Zedong did not elaborate this issue explicitly. On the other hand, we do know that Mao Zedong did not like the old Chinese culture as demonstrated in his works, otherwise he would not allow the destruction of Chinese heritages.

The real and cool fact is that it is extremely hard to change people's mind, in particular, the Chinese people's mind because our cultural tradition is so long and so strong that no one can eliminate it overnight. It is equally difficult to create a new Chinese culture, for which we would arguably suggest that Mao Zedong's wife, Jiang Qing did a lot in creation of new culture.

No matter how unsuccessful in creating of new Chinese culture, the Cultural Revolution did change the face of China.

6.1. APPROACH TO CHANGING PEOPLE'S MIND

In Chapter 3, we have discussed Mao Zedong's options, which were mainly focused on how Mao Zedong could beat his enemies, and Mao Zedong's preparations before the Cultural Revolution, which were mainly focused on how Mao Zedong could avoid the China to fall into uncontrollable chaos. All these discussions are in fact not related to the culture, which termed the Cultural Revolution.

In this regard, we would be certain that Mao Zedong did have the intention to change the Chinese people's mind, otherwise the Cultural Revolution would not be such termed.

As we said in Chapter 3 that no one could deny the fact that Mao Zedong was extremely knowledgeable in Chinese history, therefore we could deduce that Mao Zedong is unsatisfied with the Chinese Culture and Chinese tradition, even looked down the Chinese Culture and Chinese tradition. Let us now provide several pieces of evidence to this deduction.

The first example would be Mao Zedong's poem, Snow, which reads as follows:

Snow (February 1936)

North country scene:
A hundred leagues locked in ice,
A thousand leagues of whirling snow.
Both side of the Great Wall
One single white immensity.
The Yellow River's swift current
Is stilled from end to end.
The mountains dance silver snakes
And the highland charge like wax-hued elephants.
Vying with heaven in stature.
On a fine day, the land,
Clad in white, adorned in red,
Crows more enchanting.

This land so rich in beauty
Has made countless heroes bow in homage.
But alas! Qin Shihuang and Han Wudi
Were lacking in literary grace,
And Tang Taizong and Song Taizu
Had little poetry in their souls;

> That proud son of Heaven,
> Genghis Khan,
> Knew only shooting eagles, bow outstretched.
> All are past and gone!
> For truly great men
> Look to this age alone.

In this poem, we can see that Mao Zedong had a low opinion on almost all the great and famous emperors in Chinese history, and we also should not forget the time that Mao Zedong wrote this poem. It was written in 1936, when the Chinese Red Army just finished the Long March, the goal to overthrow the Kuomintang (Nationalist Party) government was very far away from the reality looking like a daydream. If Mao Zedong had such a great ambition in such a very difficult time, then what ambition Mao Zedong would have after the creation of People's Republic of China. Thus, we would not be surprised to see and understand that Mao Zedong would have the ambition to use the Cultural Revolution to change the Chinese people's mind, even create a new Chinese culture.

At this time, let us review which approach was used to change the Chinese people's mind, (i) the publication of Mao Zedong's work and its massive distribution, and (ii) the Red Guards fought old thoughts, old culture, old custom, and old tradition, these coined as four olds were actually old Chinese thoughts, old Chinese culture, old Chinese custom, and old Chinese tradition.

Nevertheless, the aim of these activities was clearly to create new Chinese thoughts, new Chinese culture, new Chinese custom, and new Chinese tradition. In this view, we could suggest that the Cultural Revolution was really well-designed because Mao Zedong had systematically consider not only how to wipe out the whole generation of career bureaucrats but also how to wipe out old Chinese thoughts, old Chinese culture, old Chinese custom, and old Chinese tradition, and to create new Chinese thoughts, new Chinese culture, new Chinese custom, and new Chinese tradition.

However, no one had defined how we should deal with the old Chinese thoughts, old Chinese culture, old Chinese custom, and old Chinese tradition, therefore the Red Guards, not fully educated but passionate teenagers, dealt with the Chinese heritages without mercy (see also, Chapter 11).

6.2. CREATION OF FOUR NEWS

Certainly, it was easy for Red Guards to destroy the old Chinese thoughts, old Chinese culture, old Chinese custom, and old Chinese tradition, but it was very hard for Mao Zedong to create new Chinese thoughts, new Chinese culture, new Chinese custom, and new Chinese tradition although Mao Zedong might systematically consider these issues in great details.

Perhaps, Mao Zedong deeply felt that the old Chinese thoughts, old Chinese culture, old Chinese custom, and old Chinese tradition could not be suited for the People's Republic of China, but more suited for a feudal China rather than a socialist China.

Now let see how the Cultural Revolution attempted to create new Chinese thoughts, new Chinese culture, new Chinese custom, and new Chinese tradition.

For the creation of new Chinese thoughts, the measure was very simple. It was to use the Mao Zedong's thoughts to replace all the old Chinese thoughts, which led to massive production and distribution of Mao Zedong's work. Still, people needed to study Mao Zedong's work and wrote their own understanding and their own application of Mao Zedong's thoughts to any concretely practical problems. Honestly and objectively, all these measures could be considered historical and phenomenal. This is so because any previous government in the Chinese history might have asked the Chinese people to study the Chinese sages' thoughts, but did not ask the Chinese people to apply these sages' thoughts to any concretely practical problems.

The measure, which required the Chinese people to apply Mao Zedong's thoughts to real-life problems, could be considered useful because the Chinese people in general could be considered to be far more interested in empty words and far less interested in actions. However, the creation of new Chinese thoughts was fatally not successful not only because a single person's thoughts could not replace all the Chinese thoughts but also the world demands diversities.

For the creation of new Chinese culture, we should say that Mao Zedong's wife, Jiang Qing, put her most energy into this activity during the Cultural Revolution. Doubtless, Mao Zedong assigned this job to his wife, Jiang Qing, perhaps because she was an actress in the past, and also perhaps because Jiang Qing talked about her ambition to create the new culture many times with Mao Zedong during the Yan'an time. The definition of culture should include too many things developed over thousands of years, unfortunately, Jiang Qing with her handful associates could not use ten years to develop a new culture, which should not only occupy the Chinese people's mind, but also totally replace the old Chinese culture.

Nevertheless, the creation of new Chinese custom and new Chinese tradition appeared far much weaker in comparison with the creation of new Chinese thoughts and new Chinese culture. This failure could be more or less related to our Chinese characteristics. That is to say that we, the Chinese people, are weak in exactly and clearly cut-off definition, with which the Chinese people are likely to do things better than other nationals in most cases, but the Chinese people would do things according to their interpretations and imaginations if there would be no very clear definition on what it means, what it interprets, what it does, etc.

Finally, if we would like to summarize the effect of creation of new Chinese thoughts, new Chinese culture, new Chinese custom, and new Chinese tradition during the Cultural Revolution, it seemed to be relatively successful during that period of time because almost each and every Chinese studied the Mao Zedong's thoughts, sang the revolutionary model Peking operas, each and every Chinese dressed similarly without distinction, and old Chinese tradition was generally abandoned.

6.3. NEW EDUCATIONAL SYSTEM

As we have mentioned several times (also see Section 5.2, Chapter 5), Mao Zedong was certainly not satisfied with the Chinese educational system. Therefore, an important goal would be to create a new educational system when Mao Zedong designed the Cultural Revolution.

Arguably, the reform of Chinese educational system was more systematical than the reform of Chinese administrative system. It is to say so, because the reform of Chinese educational system crossed the whole educational system from the primary school to university, crossed the whole curricula, and crossed the whole evaluation system from entrance to graduation.

Perhaps, the most notable measure was to let workers, peasants and soldiers go to the university to have educations without passing the severe and strict entrance examinations. The other notable measures included to send the students aged from primary school to university to countryside and factory for a short-term physical work.

At this moment, we have no way to know Mao Zedong's real intention in doing so, if he wanted to change our Chinese single-cultured tradition, it could be a right way. This is so because we, the Chinese people, in fact suffer a lot from our single-cultured, single-aimed, single-minded system.

However, the creation of new Chinese educational system failed due to the reasons, which we could not figure out so far.

6.4. ALTERNATIVE OUTCOMES

Now we look at whether the history would be different if a different person would have the chance to run the Cultural Revolution or China in a different way. Of course, this could be only the imaginary event or daydream, but there could be a tiny and slight possibility of occurrence because many people deemed to suggest that we would have a better China if the Cultural Revolution would produce a different result, of course, the people with such dream are mainly armchair commentators and post-rationalists. It is no question that a different result should be reached by a different person other than Mao Zedong, however this person must have an equal power as Mao Zedong once had, otherwise this person would be a purely powerless daydreamer.

The first opportunity to change the course of the Cultural Revolution would be that Lin Biao would have successfully assassinated Mao Zedong around 1970 to 1971. This would certainly create a totally different scenario, because the main designer of the Cultural Revolution would have gone. This situation would not be the situation that the Chinese people hoped during 1970 to 1971 although many Chinese people now pay much sympathy to Lin Biao without the consideration of his assassination plan and his escape to the USSR. This again demonstrated how we, the Chinese people, are unprincipled people (also see, Chapter 11). This is so because any similar case in world history would immediately be condemned as the highest treason, while currently many Chinese people seem to praise this treason either unintentionally or intentionally.

In the disclosed Lin Biao's plan after his death, Lin Biao and his associates did not indicate explicitly and clearly what they planned to do after killing of Mao Zedong, so we have no ideas to know how they would deal with the Cultural Revolution.

Let us go along this line a little bit far: Doubtless Mao Zedong's assassination would enrage all the Chinese people, as a legitimated heir, Lin Biao should try his best to find the scapegoats, who would be assumed to have assassinated Mao Zedong. This would lead a huge purge in Chinese military and high ranked officials. However, even these measures could not clam down the outrage and anger represented in ordinary Chinese people, so there would be a good probability to see a Chinese Red Terror. Clearly, the armchair commentators and post-rationalists have yet to consider this certain scenario.

Of course, the Cultural Revolution would be finished anyway. After this predictable purge, China would return to her normal life. However, it would be suggestive that Lin Biao has no strong experience in civil administration, and knows little about how to build an economically strong China. Of course, it would be the best case that Lin Biao would leave the daily administrative job to Zhou Enlai and Lin Biao would continue his long-term medical treatment.

On the other hand, Lin Biao's experience in the Soviet Union would lead to sharply improve the Sino-Soviet relationship, which certainly would change the China's isolation position, and be good for Chinese industry and Chinese people. However, it is still beyond our imagination of the impact of this new relationship on the enterprise of international communism.

A strong unknown factor in this power shift would be the Lin Biao's son, Lin Liguo, because Lin Liguo was very different from other Chinese leaders' sons. It was Lin Liguo who played an important role in the plan to assassinate Mao Zedong, and what role Lin Liguo would play in Chinese political stage and military stage in post-Mao Zedong era is completely unknown.

Another possible scenario would be that Mao Zedong would die earlier than 1976 but later than 1971, which was the year when Lin Biao died. The political power would doubtless move to Zhou Enlai, which would be the best scenario for Chinese people, because Zhou Enlai would stop the Cultural Revolution and focus on the Chinese economic development. The relationship between China and the US would improve faster and more rapidly than we have seen the relationship improvement in early 70s of last century. This is so because many hardliners have been literally wiped out from Chinese political system during the Cultural Revolution.

However, the unknown fact for this scenario would be how Zhou Enlai would deal with the Gang of Four. For Lin Biao, he would simply kill the Gang of Four without mercy, but this was not Zhou Enlai's style. Therefore the question remained open would be what role the Gang of Four would play under Zhou Enlai's leadership. Following this open question, then we should ask whether Zhou Enlai would be powerful enough to defeat the powerful people from Shanghai? At international stage, how the new Sino-American relationship would affect the Vietnam War and Sino-Soviet relationship would be unknown, but Zhou Enlai was in principle able to handle them because of his strong experience in international relationship. Another predictable and

natural consequence would be that Deng Xiaoping would appear earlier than
the history recorded. The new power struggle between Zhou Enlai and Deng
Xiaoping perhaps would be unlikely to occur, nevertheless the combination of
these two leaders would push the Chinese economy to move much faster. This
nevertheless would be the best alternative outcome for the Cultural Revolution
and the Chinese people.

The final but unthinkable situation would be that Liu Shaoqi would not die
so early, but Mao Zedong would die far earlier then Liu Shaoqi. This would
lead the Liu Shaoqi's liberation and regaining of his power although this
would be questionable because his potential rivals would be in power and
would do their best to silence Liu Shaoqi or prevent him from releasing from
jail. Then, the natural consequence would be that China would restart her way
abandoned during the Cultural Revolution, i.e. Liu Shaoqi's economic model.

In any these imaginable cases, the pre-condition, which would change the
cause of the Cultural Revolution and would result in an alternative outcome,
was that Mao Zedong would die earlier than his legitimated and potential heirs.
However, this was not the case at all. At Mao Zedong's position, he should
very well be informed about the healthy status of his legitimated and potential
heirs, and wisely estimate the lifespan of these heirs. This should be a strong
reason that Mao Zedong did not leave his political will on who should succeed
him, very likely because he has this answer in his mind already (see Chapter
12).

6.5. MAOISM AND INTERNATIONAL RECOGNITION

At the international level, we would say that the Cultural Revolution made
the world become familiar with Mao Zedong's thoughts, which were so called
inside China but the Maoism worldwide.

In this regards, I would say that this is an interesting phenomenon that
Maoism became world-widely recognized. This is so because we, the Chinese
people, closed the door and fully concentrated ourselves in an intensively
internal affair, the Cultural Revolution, while outside China, there was
Vietnams war, there was French students uprising, there was antiwar
movement in the US, there were economic miracles in Europe, Japan and
several southeast Asian countries, there was the Soviet invasion to
Czechoslovakia, etc. On the other hand, we, the Chinese people, ignored the
fast changing world, but were busy with Cultural Revolution. No one then,
even once dreamt the popularity of Maoism worldwide.

The popularity of Maoism could be phenomenal, and arguably the Maoism could be the only –ism named by modern Chinese people in the world [12].

To me, it is not clear what opinion the world medias and people were holding on the Cultural Revolution during the Cultural Revolution. However, the popularity of Maoism worldwide could suggest that many people around the world could hold a positive view on the Cultural Revolution at least at the beginning. Otherwise people would not be interested in Mao Zedong's book, the small red book.

Perhaps, another amazing thing occurred during the Cultural Revolution would be the so-called Ping Pong Diplomacy, which led the return of People's Republic of China back to the UN and international community. In this case, one should ask a question of whether the Cultural Revolution brought China up or down. If the Cultural Revolution would let China down, then no country would be interested in the Ping Pong Diplomacy, but simply sat to see the death of People's Republic of China.

These two phenomena would raise the strong cases against the arguments that the Cultural Revolution did nothing good and useful, even no better than doing absolutely nothing.

Chapter 7

MAO ZEDONG'S HERITAGE

Our patchwork heritage is a strength.

— *Barack Obama, Inaugural Address*

In principle, the Cultural Revolution was terminated due to the Mao Zedong's death in September 1976. Actually, the Cultural Revolution was not only Mao Zedong's experiment, but also an important experiment in human history. This experiment was related to almost all the aspects of Chinese society and Chinese people's life. No doubt, every thing remained could be considered as Mao Zedong's heritage since the beginning of the Cultural Revolution.

Thus, we might need to ask what Mao Zedong had left to China and Chinese people? This question is important because the current China is built on the aftermath of the Cultural Revolution.

After the Cultural Revolution, a new prospective China appeared in front of Chinese people, because the dull and insensitive officials had gone. After so long, we should say that a very brilliant future appeared in front of Chinese people in 1976 although we did not realize it then. Consequently, we also should say that we all currently enjoy the Mao Zedong's heritage because the Cultural Revolution opened a completely new front to the incoming Chinese leaders, mainly Deng Xiaoping. Without the Cultural Revolution, Deng Xiaoping would still be far away from the position to fully control and guide China's pathway. It would be very likely that the remained lifespan for Deng

Xiaoping would not be long enough for him to claim up the very top position without the Cultural Revolution.

On the other hand, the social system created by Mao Zedong after building of People's Republic of China and the mechanism operated by Chinese for thousands of years remained after the Cultural Revolution.

7.1. IDEOLOGICAL HERITAGE

The revolution that created the People's Republic of China was theoretically based on Marxism and Leninism because Mao Zedong's work was not yet defined as Maoism before the creation of People's Republic of China. Even Mao Zedong himself did not dare call his work as Mao Zedong thoughts (Maoism) before the creation of People's Republic of China.

Since the beginning of the Cultural Revolution, China was completely cut off from the rest of world to concentrate on our internal conflicts, although the world was changing and moving fast during 60s of last century. The real and true fact was that the Chinese people did spend a considerable time to study Mao Zedong's work during the Cultural Revolution. Of course, no any new thoughts were introduced into China from outside world during the Cultural Revolution.

However, an important fact is that Maoism is neither Marxism nor Leninism. Thus, a more important and serious question raised here is whether the Cultural Revolution changed China's face to such a degree that China is different from the socialist country defined by Marxism and Leninism. Since the end of the Cultural Revolution, Maoism was actually abandoned in China, meanwhile there were almost no political movements initiated to ask the Chinese people to read and study Marxism, Leninism and Maoism. Thus virtually we, the Chinese people, do not know what type of country China has been since the beginning of Cultural Revolution. Even we do not know what the definition of socialism is, and what is the definition of a socialist country?

This is very different from other then socialist countries, which kept a good relationship with Soviet Union, except for Albania. These countries might still have more updated concepts on Marxism and Leninism, while China left the international communist movement since the early 60s of last century. Naturally, we, the Chinese people, do not have any updated Marxism and Leninism.

Thus, the first Mao Zedong's heritage left to us is that we do not know what type of country China is according to Marxism, Leninism and Maoism. Mao Zedong left this ideological vacuum. And now we have no idea on what type of country Mao Zedong and his associates wanted to create, because we have no reference to compare with.

If we extend our view to other self-defined socialist countries around the world, we would feel that they are in the process to become countries under feudalism because the national power passes from generation to generation along a family line.

Another more or less Mao Zedong's ideological heritage would be so-called Yan'an spirit, however, the real and cool fact is that Yan'an spirit does not belong to Yan'an but belonged to the great people who once lived in Yan'an. Thus, the so-called Yan'an spirit would not play an important role in domain of ideology because their creators have gone.

7.2. POLITICAL HERITAGE

No one would deny the fact that the Cultural Revolution was a very painful and costly process, which replaced the whole old generation with the whole new generation to hold the national, provincial and local powers.

Thus, the Cultural Revolution as a massively political movement had a particular but profound impact. This impact was to replace all the leaders who still had mindsets in war with the leaders who would in very near future have mindsets for economic development. This process actually surpassed all the democratic elections in western countries, because the entire generation of career bureaucrats was mercilessly wiped out. No democratic election could ever do any similar thing to such a great degree and such a great extension in such a short time.

On the surface, the Cultural Revolution wiped out millions of career bureaucrats; in the deepest core, we understand that politicians are generally replaceable, and even all the generations of politicians are replaceable mercilessly. However, the great thinkers and great strategists are generally not replaceable because their replacement would lead a nation either to lose in dark or to fall in dark. For example, Mao Zedong was not replaceable since the creation of Chinese Communist party although his position was up and down several times. More ironically, the replacement of Mao Zedong could be one of reasons to initiate the Cultural Revolution.

Taking the damages in the Cultural Revolution into consideration, we might wonder whether China would be better if Mao Zedong was not replaced by Liu Shaoqi before the Cultural Revolution.

Similarly, Deng Xiaoping was not replaceable because his thoughts guided China since the end of Cultural Revolution although Deng Xiaoping also was up and down several times.

Of course, it is a rare case that a national leader is either a great thinker or a great strategist, thus many national leaders have no habit to sit somewhere quietly to consider how to fundamentally change their country, but are busy being involved in daily administrative jobs. Mao Zedong's political heritage simply suggests that these national leaders were replaceable.

7.3. ECONOMIC HERITAGE

The completely chaotic situation during the Cultural Revolution might imply the total collapse of planned economy, but the real fact was that the Chinese economy did not collapse although functioned very poorly. More than that, it is amazing and surprising that the salary could still be paid no matter in whole or in part during the chaotic period of the Cultural Revolution.

In a very deep sense, this indicates that the so-called planned economy might be independent of planners. In other words, the Cultural Revolution demonstrated how a planned economy could work without planners. Perhaps, it was only Deng Xiaoping who could find this deep insight on planned economy, thus he could initiate the reform in China without fear of collapse of planned economy.

7.4. CAREER HERITAGE

During the Cultural Revolution, the normal promotion along the career ladder was stopped. Literally, all the people, workers, administrative officials, teachers, army officers, still held their rank defined before the Cultural Revolution. That is to say, if someone was an associate professor before the Cultural Revolution, then he still held this rank after 10-year long Cultural Revolution, moreover, his salary was the same. This means that the Cultural Revolution froze the movement along the career ladder as well as along the salary ladder.

No one knows whether Mao Zedong deliberately did so or whether Mao Zedong had considered this issue or whether Mao Zedong did not pay any attention to such a small issue compared with other issues.

It is certain that a small portion of whole Chinese population, perhaps less than five percent, got a good chance during the Cultural Revolution, and they took the fast track along the career ladder. For example, Zhao Ziyang could be considered as such a lucky guy to get in fast track in career ladder.

Thus, the Mao Zedong's heritage for people going along the career ladder is very simple, that is, they buried their 10-year life irreversibly, but there were few front runners.

On the other hand, people might understand that they could live and work without career bureaucrats. This is the base for self-employed in this reform ear.

Chapter 8

A DIFFERENT REVOLUTION

The revolution is not a dinner party.

―*Mao Zedong*

The above citation is perhaps mostly widely cited sentence regarding what was done during the Cultural Revolution [13]. Literally, the original Chinese language of this sentence is somewhat slightly different from this version of translation although this translation is correct and loyal.

It could be interesting and useful to mention this slight difference in the above translation in order to understand our Chinese thoughts. The original saying could be literally translated in such a way with exact word-to-word translation: "The revolution is not to invite guests and not to have a meal." In Chinese pronunciations, they are Ge Ming Bu Shi Qing Ke Chi Fan, in Chinese pronunciation.

In current China, this Mao Zedong's famous saying has mutated to such a way: "The revolution is either to invite guests or to have a meal," whose Chinese pronunciations are Ge Ming Bu Shi Qing Ke, Jiu Shi Chi Fan, in Chinese pronunciation. The underlined comma and two Chinese characters are the mutations. This mutation is related to the fact that nowadays more and more Chinese people go to restaurants to have their meals, especially the career bureaucrats use the public money to have meals.

On the other hand, we can see the definition of revolution can be either brutal or entertaining and funny in Chinese sense and Chinese culture.

So the Cultural Revolution is very different from previous revolutions either in the Chinese history or in human history.

8.1. REASON FOR REVOLUTION

In the Chinese history, if we use the overthrowing of a government or organized uprisings as the standard to define a revolution, then we would find that the main cause of most revolutions is generally due to the severe shortage of food for ordinary people, especially for peasants. Therefore, the Chinese people have to choose either to die in revolution or to die in famine although they generally leave their fate to die in famine [14]. In other words, the basic hope for life and survival initiated all the previous revolutions in China either successfully overthrowing the old dynasty or unsuccessfully.

In this context, the Cultural Revolution is the revolution that has nothing to do with famine and nothing to do with survival, but purely for a revolution, i.e. a revolution for revolution.

This is certainly different from all previous revolutions occurred in China, but also different from many previous revolutions occurred worldwide. This is indeed the Mao Zedong's creation and invention, i.e. Mao Zedong chose the means of revolution to wipe out the entire generation of career bureaucrats.

8.2. UNARMED REVOLUTION

Theoretically, the Cultural Revolution is an unarmed revolution, which is very different from almost all the other revolutions in the world, although many people claimed the victims of Cultural Revolution and many people died. Of course, there were small or limited scale armed conflicts during the Cultural Revolution, but this was still a totally unarmed revolution because there were no civil war, no systematic maneuvers of armed forces, no military fronts, no heavy weapons used, and so on and so forth. In short, people were not organized to arm themselves.

The Chinese history shows that any military revolution generally takes several decades to overthrow either a previous government or a previous dynasty, and then becomes successful. On the contrary, the Cultural Revolution almost instantly destroyed the whole administrative systems in China, and made millions of career bureaucrats out off their powerful positions.

Literally, the Cultural Revolution was in fact the process of overthrowing of old government. A very common say during the Cultural Revolution was to seize the power, i.e. overthrow authorities at different administrative levels.

Of course, the real difference between the Cultural Revolution and the previous revolutions is that almost all the historical revolution was initiated from people without power, from the grassroots, from lowest social classes, and from poor people. But the Cultural Revolution was initiated from the highest ranked statesman. This is very much different because almost all the statesmen hope their country to be stable, especially in China, while Mao Zedong hoped to the chaotic situation, as he said, "some places appear very chaotic, however it is in fact the chaos in enemy side and the revolutionary masses get trainings." Can this not suggest that Mao Zedong is a really exceptional revolutionary?

8.3. TEENAGERS' REVOLUTION

Another real difference between the Cultural Revolution and all the previous revolutions is that the Cultural Revolution was a teenagers' revolution. This is so because the main force that Mao Zedong used at the first stage of Cultural Revolution was the Red Guards, who were mainly the students from middle schools and less than 18-year old.

Almost all the stories and memories related to the Cultural Revolution were mainly directed to the phase when the Red Guards executed their brutal behaviors. Actually the real revolution could only be related to this phase of the Cultural Revolution when millions of students from middle schools left their classrooms and rushed into the Chinese society. After this phase, more exactly after sending Red Guards to the countryside and reopening of schools, China became relatively clam.

When we look at this Cultural Revolution now, we would be astonished because the teenagers could create such an unthinkable phenomenon, and brought so many damages to China, especially to the Chinese cultural heritages.

Arguably, no teenagers played so important and critical roles in human history either in revolution or in wars or in economy development.

8.4. EVERYONE'S REVOLUTION

As any revolution is directly related to the war, which generally can only be conducted in a part or a small part of a country in case of size of China, so generally a revolution is the job for a portion of population.

Actually, the life of many Chinese people was not touched, even not slightly disturbed, during Chinese civil wars, second Sino-Japanese War and Korean War.

However, the Cultural Revolution touched each and every Chinese person in Mainland China no matter where he/she lived, how old she/he was, what job she/he had, and even whether he/she was alive or dead. In this view, the Cultural Revolution is indeed a revolution as Mao Zedong claimed to touch the deepest part of soul.

We say so because generally the Chinese people are not particularly active in line with the government. However, this does not mean that the Chinese people go against their government or want to overthrow their government or to do harm to their government. Here, we must absolutely distinguish this Chinese behavior from political dissents. The real Chinese behavior is to concentrate on their own narrow interests and their family's narrow interests without paying any attention to what the government asks. Everyone does her/his best to take something from government to enrich her/his home and her/his family.

For simple example, before the time that China becomes rich, one could easily find bricks in each Chinese family, these brinks taken from any public construction site were used to build a small wall to hold coals in kitchen generally.

For another example, if the local government plans to use a piece of land, then the owners of land would immediately build new houses or decorate the old house on that piece of land. Their purpose is not against the government to use this piece of land, but to use their new house or decorated old house as a bargain to force the government to compensate them more. This is the way that Chinese people behave, i.e. to try her/his best to get something from this society no matter who governs.

However, this is not the general case during the Cultural Revolution either due to the fear or due to other reasons.

8.5. PEASANTS' ROLE

In any Chinese revolutions, the Chinese peasants always played a decisive role, i.e. without peasants no one can overthrow a Chinese government. In China, we can say that any war could not be successful without the active involvement of Chinese peasants. Perhaps the Cultural Revolution is the first time in the Chinese history that the Chinese peasants did not participate significantly and or were not actively organized to take part in.

As we analyzed in Section 3.5, Chapter 3, Mao Zedong did not use the peasants as the main force in the Cultural Revolution although Mao Zedong still made many decisions during the Cultural Revolution related to peasants.

For this reason, the Cultural Revolution should be regarded as a clear milestone regarding the Chinese peasants. From then on, the Chinese peasants would step by step retreat from the Chinese political platform, and their role in Chinese politics would progressively be marginal. In short, the time that Chinese peasants played an important role in Chinese politics has gone in Mao Zedong's mind. China had already advanced into the phase that a revolution no longer need to call the Chinese peasants to active participate, and the Chinese peasants as a social class began to leave their historical stage.

8.6. A SINGLE PERSON'S REVOLUTION

Without consideration of views in Chapter 12, we could say that the Cultural Revolution was a single person's revolution. The single person, Mao Zedong, used the unarmed teenagers to change the face of China, to change the mind of Chinese people, to change the traditional Chinese culture, to change the whole administrative system in China, and so on and so forth.

Most revolutions in the Chinese history were related to two parties, an emperor with the whole administrative system and ordinary peasants, while Mao Zedong as a single person went against a system, a struggle between a single person and a career bureaucratic system.

Most likely, Mao Zedong also did not consult with anyone else to plan the Cultural Revolution if we do not consider the views in Chapter 12. When looking at several important revolutions in human history, there was always a group of thinkers, who planned the revolution and conduct the revolution.

It is a man who without real power and authority uses his fame to fight against the whole administrative system with the force of ordinary young people.

In the Chinese history, it is impossible for an emperor to fight against the whole administrative system with the force of ordinary people because any emperor, who could dare do so, would be effectively and efficiently put into house arrest in most cases, or this emperor would be immediately replaced with a new emperor. This is how the Chinese feudal system worked. Of course, there was no media and communication channel at that time, which could transfer the message from the emperor directly to ordinary citizens, while Mao Zedong did find the channel to convey his revolutionary message.

Chapter 9

WHO HIJACKED THE CULTURAL REVOLUTION?

It is a fire which, when once it begins to burn, spreads in every direction, and consumes all that comes in its way.

— *Jacob Abbott, Hannibal [15]*

As we all know and agree that Mao Zedong almost did not do any day-to-day routine administrative job, therefore it is very possible that someone, a group of people, or something else could hijack the Cultural Revolution. This hijack could diverge the course of Cultural Revolution from its original aim and mainstream.

According to the popular view, one could easily raise the figure to point out that Gang of Four hijacked the Cultural Revolution and converted it into a brutal, but an unarmed civil war. One could also denounce Lin Biao for hijacking of the Cultural Revolution.

If these would be so, one would arguably suggest that Mao Zedong might not behave as bad as many popular writers and authors said because someone or a group of people hijacked Mao Zedong's Cultural Revolution.

The question is whether the hijackers made the Cultural Revolution become brutal deeds and heartless cruelties.

9.1. HIJACKERS' POWER AND AIM

In order to determine whether there was someone or there was a group of people, who could hijack the Cultural Revolution, let us first analyze the hijackers' power. This is to say what power a hijacker needed to have in order to change the course of Cultural Revolution.

During the Cultural Revolution, the only somewhat intact system, which could do something according to superiors' orders, was the Chinese army, for which Mao Zedong held the absolutely control power. Of course, Lin Biao largely shared this control power with Mao Zedong, perhaps with several other high ranked leaders such as Zhou Enlai. However, the hijack of control power of Chinese army did not seem to have much impact on the Chinese society, and to change the course of Cultural Revolution. This is so because Mao Zedong did not use the Chinese army as a main force in the Cultural Revolution and Mao Zedong deliberately kept the Chinese army in good shape (also see Section 3.5, Chapter 3).

Still Lin Biao did not hold a major civil position, and therefore he would have difficulties to change the course of Cultural Revolution because the Cultural Revolution mainly aimed at the career bureaucrats at various civil positions rather than aimed at the Chinese army.

Honestly and frankly, Lin Biao was a great military leader, but not an important thinker as Mao Zedong was, so he would have little impact to change the course of Cultural Revolution through his own thoughts.

Perhaps, the only significant thing, which Lin Biao did, related to culture and ideology was to abolish the ranking system in Chinese army. The abolishing of ranking system in the Chinese army could also be conceived according to Mao Zedong's idea as Mao Zedong looked down all the ranking systems.

We could not deny the fact that Mao Zedong's wife, Jiang Qing, had great influence on Chinese students during the earlier stage of the Cultural Revolution. However, this influence would vanish step by step because (i) most students, who did most harmful things at the earlier stage of Cultural Revolution, went to the countryside without any united impact on the Chinese society again; (ii) Jiang Qing's interests step by step moved to the field she was familiar with, i.e. the entertainment, in order to create Mao Zedong's new culture, which we defined as Mao Zedong's second aim for the Cultural Revolution; and (iii) the Chinese society was becoming more and more stable as the Cultural Revolution was going on, and the new social order was progressively building up.

In this regard, Jiang Qing could not hijack the Cultural Revolution herself, even with somewhat questionable support from Mao Zedong. This is so simply because Jiang Qing did not have any real power during the middle and late stages of the Cultural Revolution. At this point, it would be useful to review what the Chinese writer Lu Xun, who got strong support from Mao Zedong, wrote about the women's role in the Chinese history [16]:

> "I never believe that Zhao Jun's marriage abroad could keep Dynasty Han from foreign invasions, Mu Lan's joining army could defend Dynasty Sui, nor believe the old sayings that Dan Ji led the collapse of Dynasty Yin, Xi Shi collapsed Kingdom Wu, favorite concubine Yang led Dynasty Tang into chaos. I consider that the females absolutely have no such great power in male-dominated society, and the rise and fall of dynasty should be attributed to men. But the male authors generally put the responsibility onto females, and these authors are worthless and hopeless men."

Historically, some of these women cited by Lu Xun played their roles through their husbands. In this regard, we should wonder whether Jiang Qing, Mao Zedong's wife, was able to guide Mao Zedong, because Mao Zedong's personality was so independent.

An important thinker from Gang of Four was Zhang Chunqiao, who with his associates in Shanghai city could change the course of the Cultural Revolution to some degree because Shanghai city played a leading role during the Cultural Revolution. However, this is their only role, or more correctly speaking, they could influence the course of the Cultural Revolution, but not hijack the Cultural Revolution national wide. This is so because they did not have the controlling powers in their hands to change the course of the Cultural Revolution at national level. Still, it is more questionable whether we could call Zhang Chunqiao a thinker when we look back the history because Zhang Chunqiao could not plot against the incoming power struggle between Gang of Four and other Chinese leaders after Mao Zedong's death. Even Zhang Chunqiao and other members of Gang of Four could not be prepared for the foreseeing danger. This indeed casts a question mark on Zhang Chunqiao's ability as well as the ability of Gang of Four, and their ability to operate China.

Now let us look at the aim of the people we discussed in this section, if they could be considered as hijackers.

The Lin Biao's aim is already well documented, because he wanted to assassinate Mao Zedong due to various reasons. However, Lin Biao did not seem to have the power and means to change the course and cause of the Cultural Revolution as we have just analyzed.

The next candidate for hijacking of the Cultural Revolution was Jiang Qing. However, her aim was difficult to think out because she could not benefit too much according to her way of hijacking of the Cultural Revolution.

Then, we would guess the aim of the people from Shanghai city. Very likely, their aim could be somewhat less clear and smaller than the Lin Biao's aim.

Objectively, no one could benefit a lot by hijacking of Cultural Revolution if Mao Zedong was still alive. This situation is very different from the classical Chinese novel, Three Kingdom or Romance of Three Kingdom, where we can say Dong Zhuo successfully hijacked the plan designed by He Jin and Yuan Shao and benefited a lot (also see Section 3.1, Chapter 3).

9.2. ARE WE, CHINESE PEOPLE, THE HIJACKERS?

On the other hand, the Cultural Revolution took so long, which seemed to be beyond the time-scale designed by Mao Zedong (also see Section 3.4 Chapter 3), and was so brutal, which left so many hatreds among ordinary Chinese people. It looks like that the course and cause of the Cultural Revolution were hijacked.

Then, why the Cultural Revolution became so tragic if no one with enough power and influence would have hijacked it. Here, I would suggest that it is we, the every ordinary Chinese people, who hijacked the Cultural Revolution and made it a difficult period in contemporary Chinese history. We, every Chinese citizen, who underwent the Cultural Revolution, should hold at least a tiny responsibility for the unexpected tragedies in the Cultural Revolution. We should blame ourselves rather than anyone else.

This means that our (Chinese) thoughts, traditions, behaviors, minds, in short everything belonging to us (the Chinese people) hijacked the Cultural Revolution, and made it become so brutal, so damaging, so troubling, so disturbing, so intolerant, so ill-fated and so on and so forth. We have paid the price for ourselves.

One might argue against this statement, but blame Mao Zedong, Gang of Four, Lin Biao, and anyone else for the responsibility. However, as we have analyzed, these people could only partially hijacked the Cultural Revolution, because they had no real power and the ability to completely change the course and cause of the Cultural Revolution. Moreover, we could not find out what benefit they would get after hijacking the Cultural Revolution, whose complicity was already beyond the reach of their power, even their mental ability.

Still, if it would be true that someone, or a group of people, hijacked the Cultural Revolution, we would have expected to have more public trials on these people after the Cultural Revolution. However, the history has already shown that the only public trial was related to the Gang of Four after the Cultural Revolution. Since then, we have no more person to blame publicly. It could also be possible to open the archives of Cultural Revolution in order that historians, even ordinary Chinese people, to determine the roles of various people, who were responsible for the atrocity during the Cultural Revolution. These cases did not happen, simply because we, every Chinese citizen undergoing the Cultural Revolution, did something shameful in destroying the social and public property, our cultural heritage, etc. In short, everyone did something to escalate the chaotic situation in China. As our Chinese proverb says: "Punishment cannot be applied to everyone", so we have no way to completely reopen the archives about this period of history to look at everyone's behavior

In my previous book, China: Has the last opportunity passed by?! [12], I addressed some particular characters of our Chinese people, which make China difficult to become a world power. I will of course not repeat those analyses again, but look at another aspect of our Chinese characteristics.

Of various reasons such as the great difference between Chinese language and foreign languages, and the geographic isolation of China, our society, the Chinese society, is a single-cultured system. The meaning and understanding of our language, the Chinese language, can only be understood through the defined order, i.e. from the beginning of sentence to the end of sentence. This is very different from many other language systems. Our logic similarly always goes from the beginning to the end as the Chinese language does. Our education always teaches us to do what be taught, and we, the Chinese people, generally are single-minded people, i.e. we only have one goal at a time.

For example, once the Soviet radio ironically said that the Chinese people criticized the American imperialism to such an extent that the Chinese radio stations repeated the words, the American imperialism, once every minute when the relationship between China and US was bad; and that the Chinese people criticized the Soviet revisionism to such a extent that the Chinese radio stations repeated the words, the Soviet revisionism, once every minute when the relationship was bad between USSR and China. Nowadays, the Chinese radio and TV stations repeat the words, love and money, almost once every minute if we could do such an analysis.

These are the clear evidence to show that we, the Chinese people, are single-minded people. Moreover, there are always too few foreigners living in Chinese society to use their thoughts and cultures to affect the Chinese thoughts and culture.

In particular, the people, especially the young people grew up before the Cultural Revolution, were accustomed to the slogans, for example, "Obey what Chairman Mao tells, Do what the Chinese Communist Party asks!". Therefore, it was quite natural for middle school students to throw themselves fully heartedly into the Cultural Revolution when the Cultural Revolution began. Actually, the Chinese people would do the same even without these slogans.

I believe and observe that millions of young men and women took part in the Cultural Revolution with true enthusiasm and passion, and considered their behaviors good for China.

The natural consequence of single-cultured system is the single-valued system. With the single-valued system, the only thing that anyone can do is to please his/her superior to get promotion, thus anyone has the trend to overdo or outdo in order to make his/her superior be happy and satisfied when accomplishing the assigned jobs. Their eagerness to overdo the assigned task could well beyond the limits in their superior's mind. Our Chinese society is the positive-result-driven culture.

With respect to the Cultural Revolution, it means that if a superior ordered to detain someone, then his/her subordinates would not only detain this person, but also torture him/her cruelly. Only in this way, he/she could accomplish the job given by his/her superior better and to please his/her superior very much. The root for this sad phenomenon was that the career bureaucrats are always afraid of their superior, and try their best to please their superior.

Psychologically, the Cultural Revolution did open the eyes of youths, who were then confined to their local school, and opened a new world to all youths. Actually, many youths should feel that they missed an opportunity to take part in the revolution in second Sino-Japanese War, two Chinese civil wars, and Korean War, and missed the opportunity to create the People's Republic of China. This is so because many exciting stories and legends inspirited thousand of millions of young Chinese students as well as ordinary Chinese people. For them, the Cultural Revolution indeed provided them with the real opportunity to attend the revolution.

On the other hand, the single-cultured Chinese society created a completely dull atmosphere, but the Cultural Revolution injected the new thoughts and passion into millions of teenagers, who later on became the Red

Guards. The Cultural Revolution completely changed a dull and gray routine life into an exciting and revolutionary movement.

Actually, since the creation of the People's Republic of China, all the schools used the same textbooks, therefore, the single-cultured and single-thinking pattern could be extremely very difficult to resist to any order from top brass, but is very easy to conduct the Cultural Revolution.

It is generally said that it is very painful for the current and future young generations to know that so many veteran revolutionists, who had experienced hundreds of battles as used said, died during the Cultural Revolution.

One question, which was frequently asked after the Cultural Revolution, was why Mao Zedong did not seem to have any mercy to his old fellow-comrades, who with him shoulder by shoulder underwent through the revolutionary time. However, this could be understandable if the person, who raised this question, lived in Chinese society for years with his/her eyes opened for observation.

The real and true Chinese way is that the people generally treat their fellow-comrade purely according to their superiors' view instead of principles and instead of friendship, which is the real-life reality in any Chinese entity. In particular, if the superior shows a tiny slight dislike for a fellow-comrade or co-worker no matter intentionally or unintentionally, then almost entire workforce would turn against this fellow-comrade or co-worker, even to a far severer degree than the superior does. By contrast, if the superior shows a tiny slight favor to a fellow-comrade or co-worker no matter intentionally or unintentionally, then almost entire workforce would behave in favoring this fellow-comrade or co-worker in crazy ways. This is the very nature in Chinese society. Therefore, we could easily imagine how many Mao Zedong's follow-comrades would turn their faces away from Mao Zedong when Mao Zedong lost his power.

This demonstrates an important Chinese character: we, the Chinese people, are not principled and honored people, but behave fully according to the power, position and money no matter what society we live in. Of course, our personal hatred would not be important to guide our behavior if our superior has a different view.

Still, we cannot rule out the possibility that many local authorities killed or tortured the people, who were their own enemy, during the chaotic time of the Cultural Revolution. This is a well-known phenomenon in human history, simply because everyone could easily find an excuser and opportunity to put his personal enemy into death.

Honestly and objectively, the Cultural Revolution provided a rare opportunity for each adult to expose his/her own wild ambition, and every adult could take some advantage from the Cultural Revolution if he/she happened to be born in a right family, for example, working class, peasant, solider, etc. For these adult people, we have no way to know their final purpose, but they did either seize power or obtain the property during the Cultural Revolution. Without their brutal actions, they could not touch either power or property. So, arguably people at different levels had different reasons and motivations to conduct the Cultural Revolution as brutally as possible.

Either Mao Zedong's wife, Jiang Qing, or Lin Biao once said that you should obey the order that you can understand but you also should obey the order that you cannot understand. Historically, Mao Zedong never indicated to which brutal degree that the Cultural Revolution should be conducted. Practically, no one really knew what the Cultural Revolution meant, what the aim of the Cultural Revolution was, and what Mao Zedong's definition on the Cultural Revolution was. Hence, everyone interpreted, acted and behaved according to her/his own understanding and imagination. Here, we can raise another example on Chinese interpretation of national policy: when our co-worker reported to a local police officer that his motorbike was stolen, the police officer answered that now the Chinese government advocated harmony according to national policy thus if the police officers would find the thief then it would damage the harmony so the police officers would do nothing. This is the exact way that the Chinese people interpret any national policy either due to lazy or due to other unknown reasons.

Meanwhile, China is traditionally a country that has no law, but has the social order. However, everything should go to chaos when the social order did not exist during the Cultural Revolution.

Actually, the single-thinking system was intensified during the wartime in China, which did require the Chinese people to think how to win the war. Moreover, the Chinese philosophy is very simple indeed, that is, everything is reasonable and rightful if I am not starved to death. Thus, every brutal behavior should be reasonable and rightful during the Cultural Revolution.

On the other hand, as I wrote in Section 4.2, Chapter 4, the most hateful people in China are low ranked officials as the Chinese proverb says: the official above you one degree will press you to death, guan da yi ji yai si ren, in Chinese pronunciation. These officials are not responsible for the people under their charge but responsible for their superiors because they are not elected by people but are appointed by their superiors.

In China, the reality is that these low ranked officials create most of social injustices. Thus, the Cultural Revolution did provide a good way for ordinary Chinese people to rebel their superiors, and revenge their previous injustices.

All these mentioned above could intensify the brutal degree during any political movement, especially the Cultural Revolution, in China.

Chapter 10

LESSONS TO LEARN

The Constitution, on this hypothesis, is a mere thing of wax in the hands of the judiciary, which they may twist and shape into any form they please.

—*Thomas Jefferson to Spencer Roane, September 6, 1819*

The number of people involved in the Cultural Revolution perhaps was not far less than the number of people involved in World War II, or to a less degree, in World War I, although the Cultural Revolution was confined inside Mainland China. Such a scale unarmed political movement should be the largest one in human history.

Nevertheless the Cultural Revolution is very well worthy being studied, no matter of whether it reached the predefined aims or not. Naturally, there are many lessons we can draw from the Cultural Revolution at various levels. However, we are here only to concentrate on three lessons.

10.1. CHINESE YOUTHS' ROLE

The most important, most painful and unhappiest lesson drawn from the Cultural Revolution should be that every rationale man and woman should cry for the Chinese youths, teenagers and youngsters, mainly students either from middle schools or from universities, even we can include the children, boys and girls, from primary schools into our considerations.

Their fate deemed to be the political tool used in internally political struggles, they were the political toys in various conspiracies, and these youths were brutally abandoned completely after reaching the predefined political goals.

The popular views after the Cultural Revolution are to condemn the Red Guards for their lawless behavior in the Cultural Revolution, while actually these Red Guards are truly victims of the Cultural Revolution, but not troublemakers. Each and every Chinese family actually wept deeply with tears for the fate of their children and youths, who worked in remote countryside inside China without any hope to come back to their parents. Personally, I was still too small to be a Red Guard at the beginning of the Cultural Revolution, and still I am the only child in my family, so I had no duty to go to the countryside. Therefore, my view would not be biased because I had no experience in these aspects.

Arguably, the students' movements were highly likely to be short-lived, not only because the students do not have clearly political views but also because the enthusiasm in youths came fast but extinguished fast too. The human history does not show the general phenomena or general trends that students' political movements can easily overthrow any governments, while the history did show the general phenomena or general trends that peasants, industrial workers and army's movements can overthrow the governments with hard and costly struggles.

If the human history is indeed so, then Mao Zedong would very well understand that there would be no chance that the Chinese government would be overthrown by students' political movements. Thus, the use of Red Guards would be far less danger and safest than the use of the Chinese peasants although the Red Guards created so many troubles in the life of ordinary Chinese people and in Chinese society.

In fact, the contemporary Chinese history, even modern Chinese history shows that the Chinese students were the main force for three political movements in China, (i) the May Fourth Movement (1919), (ii) the Cultural Revolution (1966-1976), and (iii) the June Fourth Tiananmen Incident (1989).

The direct lesson from these political movements demonstrated that the Chinese students are very naive not only because they put their whole enthusiasm into these moments, but also because they do not know that they are simply political tools and toys. Although there were many brilliant and talent young men or women in Chinese history, their roles were mainly limited to romantic poetry. To the best of my knowledge, no Chinese young men or women proposed any really breakthrough political theory related to social justice [12]. If this history would be so, then what the Chinese students advocated during their political moments is what they just learned or heard in their classroom from their teachers.

If we take a careful look at the Chinese youths, we should divide them according to age of eighteen, which is the normal standard for political vote. Before the Cultural Revolution, the Chinese youths beyond the age of eighteen could have no way to express their political view. This should be a lesson to be learned although there was a Hundred Flowers Movement (Hundred Flowers Campaign, 1956-1957) in China, the aim was directed to the audience elder than university students, whose age was far beyond eighteen. Another lesson is how to deal with teenagers, whose age was below the legal age for political vote. These teenagers as we mentioned several times were main force of Red Guards.

Clearly, a systematical approach should be adopted in order to restrict the teenagers' political behavior because they are not entitled the political judgment.

In a far much deeper view, the naivety of Chinese students suggests the radical problem in our Chinese educational system (also see Section 11.2, Chapter 11). Thus, if we consider the naivety of Chinese educational system and its product, the Chinese students, arguably the Chinese students at university still do not have a full picture on politics. Any political movement with involvement of Chinese students would certainly fail.

10.2. JUDICIARY SYSTEM

The application of teenagers, Red Guards, as a main revolutionary force in the Cultural Revolution was indeed Mao Zedong's great creation. We should ask whether there were no other law enforcements to execute the laws in China so that Mao Zedong had to use the teenagers to execute the laws? If the answer is yes, then we should ask why Mao Zedong did not use the law enforcement such as policemen and judiciary system, but used the teenagers? If the answer is no, then we would ask why Mao Zedong did not establish such a judiciary system after the creation of People's Republic of China?

The Chinese history really indicated that Mao Zedong and his associates created a judiciary system after the creation of People's Republic of China. However this judiciary system clearly was not aiming at the enemies that Mao Zedong defined for the Cultural Revolution. Thus, this judiciary system should be useless and worthless for Mao Zedong himself and his aim, thus Mao

Zedong launched his Cultural Revolution, because we could remember the slogan during the Cultural Revolution saying: "Smashing of public security, prosecute system, and courts", zai lan gong jian fa, in Chinese pronunciation.

Along this line of thought, the use of teenagers to replace the normal law enforcement suggests either that the Chinese laws were limited in their applications or there were no ways to deal with Mao Zedong's enemies through the normal law enforcement. Thus a more serious question raised from here is whether the Cultural Revolution launched by Mao Zedong was illegal? We have no way to answer this question because the Cultural Revolution was a political movement, which should not be related to civil codes. On the other hand, we have no knowledge of whether the Chinese Communist Party or the National People's Congress approved the launching of Cultural Revolution?

Also, there were not seem to have too many counter-measures against the Cultural Revolution (also see Chapter 4). Likely the Cultural Revolution seemed to be rationale at that stage without knowing whether it was legal or illegal.

However, the Red Guards behaved too lawlessly that everyone should feel regret why we did not use a law enforcement rather than lawless Red Guards. The lawless Red Guards and revolutionary mass confiscated personal properties, detained persons without trials, tortured millions of innocent people, and so on and so forth without even political court. All these lawless behaviors were done in the name of revolution, one might ask what was the true meaning of revolution as French revolutionist Danton once said: "Nothing is more difficult than to define a political crime". Does a revolution mean to confiscate personal properties, detain persons without trials, torture innocent people?

Perhaps, we, the Chinese people, need to explicitly define what a political crime is to avoid similar cases to happen again.

10.3. GREAT PEOPLE IN THE PAST

If we viewed the Cultural Revolution as a way to wipe out millions of career bureaucrats, it leaves us an important problem to solve. That is to say: can we have any mechanism to manage the people, who had made a great contribution in the past? Mao Zedong's way after the creation of People's Republic of China was to put the great-contributed people, mainly army officers, into the civil administrative system to become career officials. Clearly, Mao Zedong was not happy with such a solution, not only because Mao Zedong frequently said that the country and Communist Party needed new blood, but also because Mao Zedong used the Cultural Revolution to drive these career officials out from their power.

Actually, the lesson told by many officials after losing power and being brutally treated during the Cultural Revolution was that one should not work for the Communist Party.

As World War II was approaching to its end, the British people replaced Winston Churchill. Theoretically, the British people replaced the mindset of war with the mindset of economic development.

In parallel, the Cultural Revolution replaced the mindset of war with the mindset of economic development. But the difference was that the force that led to the replacement in the UK was election while the force that led to the replacement in China was the Cultural Revolution.

Chapter 11

WHY IS IT ONLY CHINA HAS SUCH A CULTURAL REVOLUTION?

There was a time when China was regarded as a Land of Opposites.

—*Giles H.A. China and the Chinese [14]*

To the best of our knowledge, there could be only three Cultural Revolutions in world history, one is the Chinese Cultural Revolution from 1966 to 1976, and then French May that was also called the Cultural Revolution occurred in 1968, and finally the Iranian Cultural Revolution from 1980 to 1987.

With this regard, the Cultural Revolution is not made in China, but also made in France and Iran. Therefore, the root of problem, which leads to the Cultural Revolution, was not limited to the single party system, but was also applied to other social systems.

Now we should ask why it is only China in all socialist countries conducted the Cultural Revolution. Although the Cultural Revolution was Mao Zedong's invention, it happened inside China, rooted from our Chinese people, rooted from our stationary thinking style.

11.1. LAW AND ORDER

The Chinese history certainly shows a painful and pitiful dilemma, that is to say, how we, the Chinese people, could use the laws to govern this country rather than use the administrative orders to govern this country although there were paper laws existed in China to some degree. In other words, China is a country with social order but without law.

Of course, it was our ancient Chinese ancestors, who decided to use the social order rather than laws to maintain the Chinese society stable. Perhaps this tradition could be rooted from the fact that our ancestors made social justice in a small village in ancient time according to the elder people, because the Chinese tradition was that young men and children should obey to their parents, who should obey their parents, grandparents, and so on. Perhaps, the stability in a family, in a village was maintained in such a manner.

In Chinese feudal dynasties, the emperors with their associates systematically made this tradition become the most important way to maintain the social stability, social justice, and civil justice. Thus, arguably we, the Chinese people, have no laws but have orders. Let us first cite the oath read by Richard I during his coronation [17]:

"(i) That all the days of his life he would bear peace, honor, and reverence to God and the Holy Church, and to all the ordinances thereof. (ii) That he would exercise right, justice, and law on the people unto him committed. (iii) That he would abrogate wicked laws and perverse customs, if any such should be brought into his kingdom, and that he would enact good laws, and the same in good faith keep, without mental reservation."

We can see that the laws were mentioned twice in this oath. By contrast, I really do not know whether any Chinese emperor needed to make an oath, even they made an oath, I wonder whether they mentioned laws. So, it is clear and evident that the laws did not occupy any important position in feudal Chinese society and in the Chinese mind.

On the other hand, the Chinese people well developed an administrative system to maintain the Chinese society in good order and stability. This administrative system was in fact operated by the millions of career bureaucrats, who maintained the social order in Chinese society for thousands of years. The fact that the feudal Chinese society could exist for so long could be mainly attributed to these career bureaucrats, who maintained social and civil justices at various levels of local authorities. In this way, the ordinary Chinese people got the protection from the career bureaucrats.

These career bureaucrats decided the judicial cases mainly according to their moral standards rather than the paper laws. Perhaps this is a main reason of why the feudal government spent so many efforts to find the career bureaucrats through very strict examinations. Thus, the feudal Chinese society had a very complicated examination system in order to find out the elite candidates for career bureaucrats, who execute the social and civil justices.

This order or the social stability was maintained by career bureaucrats, whose thoughts decide the fate of millions of ordinary Chinese people. This means that it is the politicians or career bureaucrats who decide what is right and what is wrong, but not the social justice that decides what is right and what is wrong in China.

On the one hand, the millions of career bureaucrats maintained the stability in Chinese society. On the other hand, they were the cause for our Chinese single-cultured, single-aimed and single-valued system, because these career bureaucrats passed the similar examinations from generation to generation. This could be the reason of why Mao Zedong would like to destroy the whole generation of career bureaucrats and the Chinese educational system.

Perhaps, this model was very well suited to the feudal Chinese society, where peasants conducted all the productive and commercial activities without many interventions from career bureaucrats in most cases. But this model became weak and weaker in modern society, where almost all the career bureaucrats concentrate their efforts on economic development, while the civil justice and social justice became a blinded spot for Chinese society.

11.2. OUR EDUCATIONAL SYSTEM

The lesson from the role of Chinese students in the Cultural Revolution and other Chinese political movements (also see Section 10.1, Chapter 10) suggests that the Chinese educational system is very naive, because its educated students are very naive without any clearly defined political agenda, but serve as a political tool and toy. This furthermore specially suggests that the Chinese teachers are totally naive.

This implication is very plausible because historically China did not have any massively educational system until the creation of People's Republic of China. In feudal China, the education was generally conducted in very much small scale, even mainly individually. The aim of education in feudal China was very clearly defined, that was to prepare the pupils for various examinations at local, provincial and national levels in order that the students could become career bureaucrats to govern the judiciary system in a local government. This feudally educational system created the single-aimed and single-minded educated Chinese intellectuals, who when becoming teachers, once again strengthened our single-cultured tradition.

The massively educational system built after creation of People's Republic of China focused on ordinary people, and therefore theoretically the education in Chinese middle school plays an extremely important role in the Chinese people's whole life.

In Chinese educational system, the middle school educational system plays an unimaginable and decisive role in young Chinese people. This is so because there are uncountable numbers of middle schools in China. This is so because more importantly the Chinese youths after graduated from middle school, practically, they no longer have any big difficulties in their student life, even social life. If anyone has a chance to talk with a Chinese student, even a modern Chinese man/woman, everyone would say how he/she worked hard in middle school in order to pass the national university entrance examinations. For them, the education in middle school is not forgettable in any case.

On the other hand, our educational system in middle school is a completely close-system. This is so because almost all the teachers in middle school are graduates from normal universities or educational colleges. The life of these teachers is very simple, from primary school to middle school as students, from middle school to normal university or educational college as students, from normal university or educational college to middle school to become teachers. They practically and literally do not enter into the complicated Chinese society, their life is simple in comparison with social changes, their thoughts are simply to repeat the second-handed knowledge, their aim is to educate the students to pass the examinations, and their only limited experience is related to school. This is a completely closed system because these teachers do not enter into the Chinese society at all. In this view, this exam-driven middle school system and primary school system are not greatly different from the educational system in feudal China.

Under such an educational system, most unfortunately, the Chinese students can only fatally become the political tools and toys either for politicians or for naive teachers, become the unlimited consumers for capitalists who sell various products to improve students' ability to pass the examinations, and become the hostages kidnapped by teachers of middle school and primary school in order to blackmail their parents to pay unreasonably high tuition fee.

11.3. OUR NARROW INTERESTS

Honestly, as a Chinese myself, I would say that the Chinese people are far more interested in every and each aspect in inter-personal relationship, which can include, for example, how to behave among people in order to get a favor, how to balance yourself with others, how to not hurt others while taking advantages, how to pretend knowing nothing but play a unconstructive role, and so on and so forth. This list can be very, very long. In this very fact, the inter-personal relationship is the subject that most Chinese people very much like talk and discuss.

In general, the Chinese people also are very much interested and zealous in finding out who is the leader's favorite and who is not in any entity. If now anyone goes to any Chinese bookstore, he/she certainly finds many books on how to best behave in sense of inter-personal relationship. Actually, there are uncountable books from ancient Chinese sages to modern writers to teach the ordinary Chinese people how to become a right man, zuo ren, in Chinese pronunciation.

This means that it is very hard for Chinese people to learn anything difficult and serious such as natural sciences and foreign languages, but it is very easy for Chinese people to learn and consider these soft subjects, which can be explained from each aspect of rationale, but have no definite answers.

We should also say that Chinese's interests rarely go beyond Chinese borders. Actually we are not the national who has the world view. We can compare the American films with Chinese films, where we would find the huge difference between Chinese thoughts and American or European thoughts, if we can regard the films as a representative of national characters. We can see the endless struggles, love affairs, fighting, conflicts and wars confined in Chinese territory in Chinese films, whereas we can see how the Americans conquer the universe fighting with extraterrestrial intelligent beings.

Besides, the Chinese history could be considered as a history of civil wars, because the Chinese army has fewer chances to fight beyond the Chinese borders. Either Chinese army or riots or revolutions fight within Chinese borders, and the Chinese films also happily describe the civil wars. Thus, the Chinese people have far less united willing and force, and the Chinese society has no strong gravity, which would be possible to attract all the Chinese people besides money in long-term trend. The damage of civil wars on countrymen's mind can also be read in western literature [18]:

"when he fights against his countrymen in a civil war, he abhors and hates with unmingled bitterness the traitorous ingratitude which he thinks his neighbors and friends evince in turning enemies to their country. He can see no honesty, no truth, no courage in any thing they do. They are infinitely worse, in his estimation, than the most ferocious of foreign foes. Civil war is, consequently, always the means of far wider and more terrible mischief than any other human calamity."

It is because our Chinese people have a very narrow interest confined inside China, thus actually we would like to see the intensive fights between Chinese people with most brutal cruelty.

Hence, although the Cultural Revolution was not an open civil war and not an armed conflict, the hatred between different groups and between two lines and between different parties was not less intensive than a really civil war.

In Chinese history, all the state heads are not fighters or warriors, and they are not great at military skills. This is totally different from the European history at least. For example, we can see the statesmen with great military and combat skills in historical figures such as William the Conquer, Julius Caesar, Hannibal, Richard I, Napoleon Bonaparte, etc. The real fighters in the Chinese history generally become either warlords or civil administrators. This is also particularly important because the human history seems to show that a real warrior is more likely to forgive his enemy, while a person with civil duty is unlikely to forgive his enemy. If this would be so, then we could understand another reason for the brutal behavior in the Cultural Revolution.

All in all, we can see two important Chinese characters: (i) the Chinese people obey, submit and knee down to their ill fate, and (ii) the Chinese people have great difficulties to organize themselves to defend their common interests. Certainly, Mao Zedong knew these two Chinese characters so well that he had no fear to launch the Cultural Revolution, which changed the fate of almost every Chinese person living in the Mainland China.

Likely, our narrow interest and our single-cultured society lay the foundation for our endless internal fight.

11.4. POSITIVE FEEDBACK SYSTEM

We could say that the Chinese society with her single-cultured, single-valued, single-aimed and single-minded characteristics was a positive feedback system. According to Wikiepdia [19], the positive feedback system is a system exhibiting positive feedback, in response to perturbation, acts to increase the magnitude of the perturbation.

With this positive feedback system, everything should be overdone, which would lead the Cultural Revolution to be particularly brutal and lawless. Therefore, the popular view on any social issue is fully dependent on that who is in power.

In this positive feedback system, everything, each thought, each movement, every project, in short, everything related to our life should be overdone in order to fully finish the job. If we, the Chinese people, cannot overdo assigned job, then we will abuse and misuse something in order to overdo the job although the misuse and abuse are different from overdoing, they are particular characteristics of our Chinese people.

Thus, we could see too many cases of abuse and misuse in policy. For example, when Mao Zedong reopened the university for experienced peasants, workers, and soldiers, we then could see the hero in that time, Zhang Tiesheng, who was not able to write a single answer to the problems in university entrance examinations but entered the university as a hero. Actually every Chinese can raise many examples on how we overdo, abuse and misuse some policy, in more deep sense, every Chinese has certainly overdone, abused and misused some order from his/her superior or policy unintentionally.

Chapter 12

CAN CONSPIRACY THEORY WORK FOR CULTURAL REVOLUTION?

> *In a word, it was a case of what is called political necessity; that is to say, a case in which the interests of one of the parties in a contest were so strong that all considerations of justice, consistency, and honor are to be sacrificed to the promotion of them. Instances of this kind of political necessity occur very frequently in the management of public affairs in all ages of the world.*
>
> —*Jacob Abbott, Hannibal [15]*

Up until now, our analysis goes against the simple-minded and childish explanations on the cause and course of the Cultural Revolution, and our analysis on the Cultural Revolution is absolutely concentrated on Mao Zedong's activities and options. Our analysis clearly and evidently showed that the Cultural Revolution is a well-designed and well-controlled process.

Actually, China is the place where the random event occurs very rarely, therefore any social and political movement inside China should be considered as a deliberate action with certain deep background, while any deliberate action or movement with the scale of Cultural Revolution should be designed by super-wise people as Mao Zedong himself. In other words, any unexpected events could be due to conspiracy.

Based on such a well-designed and well-controlled process, now let us look at the Cultural Revolution into anther deeper level, i.e. now we ask (i) whether a group of people initiated the Cultural Revolution under the name of

Mao Zedong, (ii) whether the Cultural Revolution was the masterpiece of some hidden force who could influence Mao Zedong's thought in various ways as we know that Mao Zedong had many options before the Cultural Revolution, and (iii) whether someone together with Mao Zedong plotted the Cultural Revolution with a far deep aim in their mind.

In other words, we need to consider whether the conspiracy theory can explain the Cultural Revolution, and who were the fellow-conspirators.

However, one can only make such a hypothesis because any conspiracy should include extremely very few people, who might have been silenced long before, and more importantly any serious, well-designed and well-hidden conspiracy would not leave any traces for the next generations to track. Therefore, we can only apply our ability and logic to analyzing this issue with several broken lines. And we can only guess the conspiracy with respect to the aftermath of the Cultural Revolution, because the people at state level involved in the conspiracy either died earlier or would not tell anything if they are still alive.

If we look back Mao Zedong's entire life, we can easily find that Mao Zedong is a very prudent, careful, cool, persevered and analytical, but not an emotional and impetuous person. It is very hard to find that Mao Zedong did something without careful consideration, even long-term careful consideration with balance on every aspect. This is very suggestive because it once again suggests that the Cultural Revolution is not a simple torturing game, but must have a far deep reason. In this case, the conspiracy theory would work for the Cultural Revolution.

According to the conspiracy, we could arguably suggest that either Mao Zedong himself or a group of people together designed the Cultural Revolution for an untold aim.

12.1. Who had the Ability to Plot?

Actually, everyone has a certain ability to plot a conspiracy, which could arguably be a cut-off line between humans and other animals.

However the one, who masterminded a plot with the scale as large as a whole Mainland China as Cultural Revolution, should be an absolute and indubitable genius. The Chinese history clearly indicates that there are not many geniuses at such a level. This is so because the traditional Chinese plots are more related to a small-scale activity covered by various excuses without motivation of the whole nation. The plot we cited in the classical Chinese novel, Three Kingdoms or Romance of Three Kingdoms, was certainly a failed plot with mobilization of whole army (also see Section 3.1, Chapter 3).

As we said in previous chapters, anyone should agree that Mao Zedong is extremely talent if he/she would like to continue a fair discussion on this issue. Now we should search for the people, who at least have similar wisdom and genius as Mao Zedong has, thus they could work out a scheme for the initiation of Cultural Revolution, and then for the ending of Cultural Revolution.

Yet, if there would have been such a genius from grassroots in Mainland China before the Cultural Revolution, this person could make a plot as the Cultural Revolution, the big problem for her/him would be how to pass her/his plot on to Mao Zedong, who had the real power to initiate the Cultural Revolution. We have to admit that a genius, who conducted a grass-rooted life, could not present her/his plot to Mao Zedong, simply because there is no such a communication channel between ordinary Chinese people and top brass in Chinese society to present a conspiracy. Throughout Chinese history, there were several occasions that the grassroots could present their plans and ideas to emperors, however we must bear in mind that it is the emperors themselves who initiated these cases when their country and dynasty encountered some unsolved big difficulties.

In any case, no Chinese leaders theoretically had the possibility to read such a plot as Cultural Revolution before the Cultural Revolution.

Now let us see the possibility that a group of people initiated the Cultural Revolution under the name of Mao Zedong. In this case, this group of people could be a Mao Zedong's think tank. This think tank could theoretically intrigue a plot, however this possibility is unlikely because the Chinese think tank generally do not produce any new ideas besides citing the examples from Chinese history or borrowing some ideas from abroad.

The Gang of Four could not be the Mao Zedong's think tank at all not only because some of them were still unnoticeable before the Cultural Revolution, but more importantly because they lacked of support from the Chinese army and from the pioneer generation of revolutionaries. Still, Mao Zedong's wife, Jiang Qing, had no ability to contrive such a big conspiracy.

A person with Mao Zedong's ambition and experience would have a great difficulty to look at any plot as simple as a childish game. Thus the person, who could think out such a conspiracy, should win Mao Zedong's full respect with equal or somewhat equal ambition and experience as well as a very high position in Chinese Communist Party and government.

Therefore, this genius must come from the state level in China to make such a plot, and this genius could be Mao Zedong himself or anyone else who could communicate with Mao Zedong frequently and freely. The latter is very suggestive because our deduction seems to suggest that this genius should be one of Mao Zedong's fellow-comrades.

The history of Chinese Communist Party and People's Republic of China clearly shows that only two persons have such a great and talent ability to plot the Cultural Revolution because the Cultural Revolution is based on a totally new idea, which should be a revolution without civil war and without too much bloodshed.

These two great figures in contemporary Chinese history would be Mao Zedong and Deng Xiaoping. Mao Zedong created his system of thoughts as defined as Maoism or Mao Zedong thoughts, with his thought Mao Zedong established the People's Republic of China, while Deng Xiaoping initiated the Chinese reform, which put the China into the world stage.

In the history of People's Republic of China, Mao Zedong and Deng Xiaoping both were the only thinkers and strategists, whose thoughts reshaped China and shaken the world.

Both are the number one genius in modern and contemporary Chinese history, and were fully capable to plot the Cultural Revolution. In such an analysis, our analysis and inference would be totally different from ordinary accounts, which indicated that Deng Xiaoping along with Liu Shaoqi were the victims and sufferers of the Cultural Revolution.

However, the history of Cultural Revolution did show that Deng Xiaoping suffered far much less than the whole generations of leaders at the same level, most of his fellow-comrades died miserably and hopelessly. By the clear contrast, Deng Xiaoping did not suffer much physically and mentally. In fact, Deng Xiaoping successfully survived through the most chaotic period during the first phase of Cultural Revolution. Arguably, everyone, who could survive the most chaotic period during the first phase of Cultural Revolution, could survive through the whole Cultural Revolution. At Deng Xiaoping's political rank, he could be deliberately arranged to escape from the most chaotic period of the Cultural Revolution.

Another important fact was that Mao Zedong allowed Deng Xiaoping to work at the later stage of the Cultural Revolution, which is a good indicator that Mao Zedong very much trusted Deng Xiaoping.

The extremely most important point was that Mao Zedong left Deng Xiaoping alive during the Cultural Revolution. However, Mao Zedong from his personal experience through power struggle and his political instinct should well know that no one could hold the national power safely if Deng Xiaoping would be alive after Mao Zedong's death no matter what position Deng Xiaoping would hold.

This is very suggestive, because we could say that Mao Zedong obviously and deliberately left his power to Deng Xiaoping for the post-Cultural Revolution era because most importantly Mao Zedong did not leave any personal and political will before his death although he was seriously ill for a long time and would have enough time to make a political will to define who should be his heir.

Here, many simple people would indicate the fact that Deng Xiaoping lost his power twice during the Cultural Revolution, however I would remind these people the Chinese proverb, Zhou Yu beats Huang Gai, one wants to beat the other, while the other wants to be beaten. This proverb comes from the chapter 46, Using Strategy, Zhuge Liang Borrows Arrows; Joining A Ruse, Huang Gai Accepts Punishment, in the classical Chinese novel, Three Kingdoms or Romance of Three Kingdoms [20]. Wu should also recall the most famous Deng Xiaoping's quotation: "It doesn't matter whether a cat is white or black, as long as it catches mice."

If we could imagine the relationship between Mao Zedong and Deng Xiaoping as Zhou Yu versus Huang Gai, then one should ask why? Why did Mao Zedong need to treat Deng Xiaoping in such a way? What was their final aim?

12.2. REVERSED TIME AXIS

In previous chapters, our analysis goes along the time axis, that is, we followed the historical path from the time before Cultural Revolution until the time after Cultural Revolution.

In Chapter 1, we frankly and honestly admit our limited and humble ability compared with Mao Zedong and his associates, simply because we do not deny that Mao Zedong is a great genius. Then, Mao Zedong should have a certain ability to predict the future before the Cultural Revolution as a great strategist always does, i.e. the Cultural Revolution would take which course, what would be the ending point for the Cultural Revolution, and so on and so forth. But the most important issue and the bottom line should be that Mao Zedong would leave his power to whom and who would be left in the power center to guide China to go to the future after the Cultural Revolution?

Here, we must once again admit Mao Zedong's ability to predict the future. This fact can be demonstrated over entire his career before the creation of People's Republic of China. For example, Mao Zedong predicted the defeat of Nazi Germany before the battle of Stalingrad.

The key question we need to answer is who would be left in the power center to guide the Chinese people to go to the future after the Cultural Revolution?

Now, when we look back to the Chinese history after the Cultural Revolution and what happened in the later stage of the Cultural Revolution, we can easily and readily find that the only significant figure, who stayed in the power center and could guide China and the Chinese people to go to the future, was Deng Xiaoping. This once again is extremely very much suggestive.

If this is not any simple coincidence that Deng Xiaoping was left in the power center, then there should be some arrangement between Mao Zedong and Deng Xiaoping to create such a historical coincidence.

Or more openly, we would arguably suggest that Mao Zedong and Deng Xiaoping together masterminded the Cultural Revolution. This is so, because we can see almost the whole generation of politicians, generals and fellow-comrades, who followed Mao Zedong to create the People's Republic of China, at different steps of career ladder fell from their positions forever. By clear contrast, Deng Xiaoping has fallen and risen, and fallen during Mao Zedong's time, but all these rising and falling are not fatal for Deng Xiaoping, because he finally held the power to guide the future direction of China. Deng Xiaoping should be considered as the final winner of the Cultural Revolution.

The final result in power center after Cultural Revolution is neither a simple coincidence nor the God's intervention, but is the historical demand. This demand is very simple: it is not Mao Zedong's aim to eliminate Liu Shaoqi as many authors explained, but it is Mao Zedong's aim to use Deng Xiaoping to make a great China. At any rate, whether it was the original plan or not, such was the result.

12.3. FINAL GOAL OF CONSPIRACY

We can believe that Mao Zedong indeed spent most of his time to consider this country rather than other trivial issues, which can be interesting to ordinary people. Otherwise, Mao Zedong would have no need to learn

German language and searching of ancient Chinese books to find some solutions to build China.

If it is only Mao Zedong and Deng Xiaoping, who are capable to plot the Cultural Revolution, then it is natural to ask what is their final goal?

No matter how people denounced Mao Zedong and his associates for their behaviors in the Cultural Revolution, we still can believe that they hope a strong and prosperous China as all the Chinese people do. If this assumption can stand, then Mao Zedong and Deng Xiaoping should be disappointed by the economic development in relatively newly created People's Republic of China.

As we analyzed in Chapter 3, Mao Zedong's enemy is highly like to be the entire administrative system, or the whole bureaucratic systems, where the career bureaucrats occupied almost all the positions. Mao Zedong should also dislike the Chinese educational system, which produces people, whose qualification could not be suited for the proposed reform conducted by Deng Xiaoping.

Can we not say that the Cultural Revolution is to pave the path for Deng Xiaoping and his future reform? A well-designed conspiracy should leave the person, who intrigued the plot, to survive, and benefit the result of their conspiracy.

Objectively and fairly, Mao Zedong could consider that Deng Xiaoping is an ideal candidate for Mao Zedong's position after his death although Mao Zedong never said this openly. This argument is based on the following facts: (i) Deng Xiaoping has both military and civil experience, which is different from other Chinese leaders who either have strong military experience as Marshal Lin Biao or have rich civil experience as Liu Shaoqi; (ii) Arguably Mao Zedong should know Deng Xiaoping extremely very well because both experienced the Long March; (iii) Still, Deng Xiaoping has relatively richer experience abroad than other Chinese leaders; and (iv) Mao Zedong through his experience knew very well that no one could defeat Dong Xiaoping, even Mao Zedong left his power to someone else after Mao Zedong's death.

Actually the history is an unarguable case where Mao Zedong apparently left his power to Hua Guofeng, whose role seemed to be transit, i.e. to arrest Gang of Four and then to pass his power to Deng Xiaoping. As seen, the final power belonged to Deng Xiaoping.

If all these would be so, then it could suggest that Mao Zedong either got the idea from history, or from his own meditations, or from some meaningful events, or from someone's suggestions because their early conversation could influence Mao Zedong to plan the Cultural Revolution.

According to the final results in power center after the Cultural Revolution, we could say that the final goal for Mao Zedong to launch the Cultural Revolution would be to pave the way for Deng Xiaoping to hold the power, and would be to prepare the reform in China, which began from the end of 70s until now. At this level of conspiracy, they indeed need to (i) wipe out a whole generation of bureaucrats, who would doubtless go against the reform; (ii) destroy the Chinese culture, whose very nature is stable; and (iii) shaken the Chinese educational systems, whose products are examination-oriented.

The official position held by Deng Xiaoping before the Cultural Revolution was not very high, so generally no one would consider that Deng Xiaoping could hold the absolutely national power simply because many leaders were at higher positions than Deng Xiaoping was. In this view, the Cultural Revolution cleared out the pathway for Deng Xiaoping going to the highest position in China in order to accomplish his, perhaps together with Mao Zedong's, plan to reform China as Peter the Great did for the Russia.

In People's Republic of China, the only person, who has equal wisdom with Mao Zedong, would be the later Chinese leader, Deng Xiaoping. It is absolutely impossible for Mao Zedong not to notice this point.

12.4. EXTENDING OF CONSPIRACY THEORY

Along this line of thought, one could imagine that the incident occurred in Tiananmen Square in June 4, 1989 could be a somewhat lost-controlled conspiracy or not well-controlled conspiracy, which finally led the intervention from the Chinese army. By our previous analysis, it clearly showed that the Cultural Revolution was always under Mao Zedong's control without the need to call the bloody intervention from the Chinese army.

On the other hand, Deng Xiaoping clearly learned the lessons from the Cultural Revolution, where our analysis shows the only efficient and effective counter-measure against the Red Guards was the armed Chinese army (also see Section 5.1, Chapter 5).

The difference between these two events is that the aim for the Cultural Revolution was to wipe out an entire of generation of career bureaucrats, who in future would be the obstacles for the Deng Xiaoping's reform either because these career bureaucrats were hardliners or because these career bureaucrats were corrupted. By the contrast, the event occurred in June 1989 was aiming to get rid of a single person, who would be Zhao Ziyang because his reform seemed to be too bold and too fast.

If we define that Mao Zedong launched the Cultural Revolution because he felt the China's development too slower, then we could define that Deng Xiaoping would launch the mourning of Hu Yaobang to deal with a single-person enemy because he felt Zhao Ziyang's step of reform was too large for the stability of China.

Clearly, Deng Xiaoping learned the heavy lessons from the Cultural Revolution, thus he did not call the students from middle schools to come out from their classroom, used the students from universities, who were certainly more rationale than the students from middle schools. However, it almost lost the control when calling students out from their campuses, because the students without social experience were too easily to be manipulated by any irresponsible calls.

An important similarity between these two events would be that the Chinese students functioned as political tool and toy for removing of someone from political power center as we have discussed the reason for the use of Chinese students in Section 3.5 in Chapter 3.

The damage control could arguably not be well timed compared with what Mao Zedong did for Red Guards at the time when the whole China agreed that the terror created by Red Guards should be put into the end (also see Section 5.1, Chapter 5).

Chapter 13

CAN A SIMILAR REVOLUTION HAPPEN AGAIN?

Hegel remarks somewhere that history tends to repeat itself. He forgot to add: the first time as tragedy, the second time as farce.

— *Karl Marx The Eighteenth Brumaire of Louis Bonaparte (1852)*

I would not say that the future is necessarily less predictable than the past. I think the past was not predictable when it started.

— *Donald Rumsfeld, Former United States Secretary of Defense*

The two citations above indicate that it is almost impossible to predict whether a similar revolution would take place again in China, however we should try to answer this difficult question before ending this book.

This question is so important because Mao Zedong once said that the Cultural Revolution should take place not only once but several times, each for several decades. When Mao Zedong said this, he was in good health so we cannot consider this sentence as a joke or crazy words because our analysis so far demonstrated how the Cultural Revolution was well-designed and well-organized either by Mao Zedong alone or by two great geniuses in contemporary Chinese history.

Of course, a new Cultural Revolution could occur under another name if the Cultural Revolution will still be so notorious, or use of same name if the

Cultural Revolution will become bright again although it was once decided that no Cultural Revolution would be conducted in future.

Actually, all the short-term negative points, but long-term positive points in the Cultural Revolution would be the arguments to conduct the future Cultural Revolution either under the same name or other names, meanwhile all the totally negative points will certain be the arguments against the new Cultural Revolution.

Now let us look at the pro and con points for the future, and then let history decide the future path of China.

First of all, we should have no more need to define the pre-conditions for initiation of Cultural Revolution, because we have already addressed the problems in front of Mao Zedong before the Cultural Revolution, and no one would expect to see that these conditions would appear again. Second, we should also no more need to define the pattern of Cultural Revolution in order to compare the pattern in any political movement in future, because we have already gone through the Cultural Revolution along the time course.

So, we would only concentrate our efforts on pro and con points, however, we are talking about the possibility but not the certainty. The possibility of occurrence of Cultural Revolution in the future will be dependent on the balance between favored points and disapproved points in the national leaders' mind.

13.1. PROS

With our previous analysis, we could determine the very basic pre-conditions for initialization of the Cultural Revolution. This is to say, we must look at the aim of the Cultural Revolution again: if the aim once again reaps then the pre-conditions for the Cultural Revolution would be met. In such a case, the question of whether a national leader would initiate another Cultural Revolution under other names would be dependent on this leader's judgment, brevity, courage, and other factors, which restrict him.

Historically, what happened in the Chinese history would have the possibility to occur again, simply because the Chinese people cannot produce sufficient new ways to deal with old unsolved problems as well as new problems. Thus, it would be highly likely that the Cultural Revolution would be the only solution for the problems, which cannot be solved through judicial system.

Since the beginning of 19th century, the Chinese society has been changing from a stationary and closed feudal society to a society, which includes almost all fashionable and popular thoughts from major parts of the world from time to time. However, the incoming thoughts and ideas did not come from each corner of the world because the Chinese people are mainly absorbing their knowledge from English and Japanese, then to some less degree from Russian and French.

This consistent changing in Chinese popular thoughts would be the fundamental base for various revolutions occurred since 19th century in China. Until now, this process is still going on without seeing the ending point, which would be the fundamental base for various revolutions or reforms in China in any future moment. In such a case, one might ask where the ending point will be? The apparent ending point would be that the Chinese people would hold the position of thinking leaders in the world, which means that the Chinese thoughts would prevail all the thoughts around the world. However, unfortunately, we could not see any sign of such an event to occur in the near future, actually most of schools of thoughts and new ideas come from Europe and the US [12], for example, capitalism, socialism, communism, globalization, global warming, overpopulation, etc.

If China would not become the world-thinking leader, then China would always undergo the process of building of new culture, adopting of new thoughts and catching up with the popular thoughts in the world. This process might take quite long as said by Andrew Cunningham: "It takes three years to build a ship, it takes three centuries to build a tradition." On the other hand, this would plant the seed for either revolutions or reforms in the future. This is so because the dominant thoughts and ideas in a whole generation would appear useless and worthless for the next generations under the single-cultured Chinese educational system, even the knowledge structure in each generation is rather different one from another. For example, the focus of the current generation is more related to love affair and money, which are the long-term focuses of Chinese society since very early on.

An important point would be the speed that the whole generation of career bureaucrats is becoming a social class because the biggest bureaucratic system has been built in China. As a social class, whose interests would be strongly different from either the ordinary people's interests or the national leaders' interests, this would provide a strong case to wipe them out. Although these career bureaucrats are the elites passing uncountable examinations, these elites could create an inefficient as noted by Roosevelt [21]: "the Chinese had constructed an inefficient governmental system based in part on the theory of written competitive examinations." Historical experience seems to suggest that the administrative work is a black hole, which means the administrative system can be handled with a few people or unlimited people but the unlimited people still feel the need for increasing of their numbers.

If the Cultural Revolution would be the only solution for elimination of millions of career bureaucrats because their thoughts were out-of-date, then there would be a high probability for the Cultural Revolution.

Actually, the pre-condition, which leads to the Cultural Revolution, is already very clear until this point in this book. That is when the entire generation of career bureaucrats, who operate all the administrative activities, becomes complete obstacles to the national leader. Then the only way, although it is painful and chaotic, is to use a Cultural Revolution to wipe out all of them if this national leader has sufficient fame and reputation to mobilize millions of ordinary people. The human history has already shown that Stalin used the Great Purge to wipe out many career bureaucrats, while Mao Zedong used the Cultural Revolution to wipe out the entire generation of career bureaucrats.

This is the most important point to support the reoccurrence of Cultural Revolution, because China is not a very dynamic country, even a stationary country in this sense. Thus, each school of thoughts would prevail until it has to collapse, each policy would execute for a very long time without its time limit. This is simply because our single-valued system would not rend the Chinese people to have a concept to replace or reevaluate something after a period of time since its implementation, and would prefer to use it forever. As we analyzed, what the Cultural Revolution really did was to wipe out the whole generation of war-minded career bureaucrats, who had no experience to move the Chinese economy ahead. On the other hand, the Cultural Revolution is different from any reforms in terms of its mechanisms and time length. The reform wipes out unnecessary career bureaucrats step by step through a slow but somewhat less painful process, while the Cultural Revolution did this through a rapid and extremely painful process. Therefore it would be decided according to a national leader's judgment and urgency of whether it is needed to conduct a revolution or a reform.

So, the question is why we, the Chinese people, need to wipe out the entire generation of career bureaucrats, because it is extremely hard to think out an efficient and effective mechanism to wipe out an entire generation of career bureaucrats with such a size of administrative system. This is perhaps a particular Chinese characteristic, i.e. historically the Chinese people prefer a big-sized government, which is composed of elites, who pass various difficult examinations. This is a particular Chinese tradition with nothing to do with either a single-party or multi-party system.

On the other hand, a single-party system would actually use a revolution, either in forms of Cultural Revolution or others, to reach the aim similar to an election. Of course, the scope is far beyond the democratic elections in terms of number of people losing of power.

There are still several other points in favor for the reoccurrence of Cultural Revolutions in future. In particular, the Chinese system, which is a single-cultured, single-aimed, and single-valued, would provides the mechanism to do what a leader considers necessary to do. On the other hand, the Chinese constitution, social system and administrative system do not provide any efficient and effective mechanisms or legal measures to prevent a new Cultural Revolution or a political movement from happening under another name. This is so because until now we cannot answer the question of whether the Cultural Revolution was legal or illegal, and we still have no mechanism against new Red Guards. In fact, currently many poor Chinese people dream the day to confiscate the rich people's property saying that the confiscation is the revolution.

Meanwhile, a single-cultured system would provide fewer options when an unusual event occurs. Without many options, the Cultural Revolution could be an option, because it is still better than no options. With our naive educational system, there is still the possibility to occur another Cultural Revolution because the nature of students is idealist and naive although now they are no longer interested in revolution and politics.

Now let us see whether there would have been the other ways to wipe the entire generation of career bureaucrats. If we cannot figure out any alternative approaches, then the probability of occurrence of Cultural Revolution would dramatically increase. By contrast, such an probability would diminish if we could find the ways to pass by this problem.

When there is the extremely big problem between the head of state and entire administrative system or entire population of bureaucratic, this could be possible because the generation gap between state head and entire population of bureaucratic could be too large to understand, even to look at each other, then the national leader would feel that the entire population of career bureaucrats useless and worthless.

Technically, the extremely chaotic situation would be a solution to prevent career bureaucrats from organizing of fighting. Moreover, it appears that the Cultural Revolution could be only way that the zero-leveraged ordinary Chinese people could do something against their boss.

13.2. Cons

My previous analysis in this book actually conducted mainly in such a way, i.e. I listed all the problems, which I could thought out, in front of Mao Zedong, then I presented the possible solutions, finally I determined whether we, the ordinary Chinese people, would take the similar decision. If the answer would be yes, then the chance of occurrence of Cultural Revolution would greatly increase because every ordinary Chinese citizen could make a similar decision. If the answer would be no, then the chance would dramatically reduce because an ordinary Chinese citizen could not choose a similar option.

Once Lin Biao said that Mao Zedong was the person, who appeared once for several thousands of years in Chinese history. No matter how people can discredit this saying as a flatter. This saying is quite true in fact. This is so because there are very fewer thinkers in the Chinese history [12] if we examine the Chinese history in great details. Many so-called ancient Chinese thinkers and sages were in fact armchair commentators or post-rationalists. These armchair commentators or post-rationalists did not have their own original thoughts in sense of systematical thoughts related to how to exercise social justice and fair distribution of social wealth, far much worse, they did not have any experience as a national leader.

If we look back the Chinese history again, we can find that there are only three persons, who came from grassroots but created either a new dynasty or this republic. These three persons are Liu Bang, Zhu Yuanzhang and Mao Zedong. Here, many people will of course point out the names of many people originated from grassroots, who overthrow the old governments or dynasties and built a new government or dynasty in Chinese history. However, the Chinese history clearly shows that these dynasties or governments were short-lived, and these leaders were shortsighted in comparison with Mao Zedong.

In such a case, we would not expect to see that a new genius as great as Mao Zedong or Deng Xiaoping would appear very soon in China. Even, there would be such a genius very soon, whose fame and reputation would be far less than Mao Zedong's fame and reputation because the human history shows that only the first generation of national leaders have the greatest fame and reputation, which give the base to conduct such type of revolution as the Cultural Revolution.

So the first generation of national leaders, who created a new country, would have such influence to conduct the Cultural Revolution typed revolution, such as Mao Zedong and Stalin. On the other hand, the national leaders in following generations would not risk their positions to launch such a revolution although they would have the intention and need to conduct a Cultural Revolution typed revolution. In China, besides Deng Xiaoping, no national leader would have the fame as Mao Zedong to have the possibility to conduct such a Cultural Revolution typed revolution.

Even, there would be such a new genius appeared in China. However, we must admit that a Cultural Revolution typed revolution would be difficult to launch again, because the Mao Zedong's Cultural Revolution produced such a hugely negative impact that everyone would not dare do the same thing under the same name.

Another issue related to personality would be whether a national leader would have sufficient courage to launch the Cultural Revolution, because Mao Zedong and Deng Xiaoping indeed have such courage.

Yet, if we consider that the Red Guards, the main force during the Cultural Revolution, were teenagers, then the new Cultural Revolution would be indeed unlikely to occur again. This is so because China is rapidly becoming an aging country with somewhat exponential reduction of teenagers through generations. Thus, there would be less and less young men and young women to be mobilized to attend a revolution, so the children of revolution are becoming less and less. On the other hand, perhaps more important is that the students from middle schools are currently efficiently disarmed in ideology with modern luxury life. Thus their focus is no longer on the so-called revolution, but on the long-term trend in Chinese society, money and love.

Another issue against the reoccurrence of Cultural Revolution is that the statesmen currently have no time as Mao Zedong had to consider all the problems in somewhat isolated situation, so it would be difficult to have an option as Mao Zedong thought out. This perhaps is a pre-condition as Alexandre Dumas wrote [22]:

"Possibly nothing at all; the overflow of my brain would probably, in a state of freedom, have evaporated in a thousand follies; misfortune is needed to bring to light the treasures of the human intellect. Compression is needed to explode gunpowder. Captivity has brought my mental faculties to a focus."

In this view, Mao Zedong's years in seclusion since losing his power provided him with such an idea of Cultural Revolution, while Deng Xiaoping's years in exile provided him with the plan to reform China.

Yet, the fighting and conflict between ideologies would become less and less important if we do not refer this issue to religions at world stage. Even, we would refer to religions, as I wrote in the book [12]: "the Chinese people never launched any open war for the sake of religions, simply the religion for Chinese people is a way to show how we are rich and can spend money randomly". If there would not be any serious fighting in ideology then we would expect little chance to launch a new Cultural Revolution.

On the other hand, we should realize that the role of national leaders has changed very much significantly due to the fast development of science and technology. The current world leaders and national leaders spend most their time to find and create jobs for jobless people, to find markets to sell domestic products, to find investors to inject money into toxic assets, to present in various ceremonies and meetings, to issue the policies generated from other people's mind, and so on and so forth. Thus, the issue related to ideology would become less and less important.

Since the initiation of reform, the interest in Chinese people returned to their general and historical trends, which dominated the Chinese society for two thousands of years. This trend is to pursue money and love, so the Cultural Revolution is becoming less and less important. Honestly and frankly, the biggest ambition for Chinese people is to have a great house filled with various luxury items, which are mostly used only for once. Why do we need another revolution if we cannot confiscate other's property?

Chapter 14

FINAL REMARK

Providence does not allow anyone accomplish all his ambitions.

—*A quotation from a Chinese book*

No matter of whether Mao Zedong himself or Mao Zedong and Deng Xiaoping together plotted this well-designed and well-controlled Cultural Revolution, the Cultural Revolution did not meet his or their expectations and ambitions.

Did Mao Zedong make a capital mistake in launching of the Cultural Revolution? Perhaps, yes because he lost the love from ordinary Chinese people; perhaps no because his heritage gave the room for Deng Xiaoping's reform.

Was the Cultural Revolution successful? Perhaps, yes because Mao Zedong was still holding power during the Cultural Revolution; perhaps no because the Cultural Revolution has become an icon of chaos and lawlessness.

Did Mao Zedong create new Chinese thoughts, new Chinese culture, new Chinese custom, and new Chinese tradition? Most likely, no because all the olds reappear in current China; perhaps yes because Mao Zedong's thoughts become Maoism in parallel to Marxism and Leninism, which might be Mao Zedong's initial plan.

Do we have any mechanism either to promote another Cultural Revolution or to prevent another Cultural Revolution from occurring? For this, we have no answer at all.

If we expend our panorama to human history, we would find that many great historical figures did not fulfill their ambitions. For example, Richard I lionhearted did not recapture Jerusalem, Napoléon did not conquer Russia, and so on and so forth.

Perhaps, these are the role of great leaders, i.e. they created something completely new, but had limited time and limited resources to finish their job. On the other hand, if they would have finished their plan successfully and they would still had time and resources, and then the history would have given different evaluations on their role in history.

Furthermore, we could say that the next generation has the opportunity of doing great thing successfully because the previous leaders left sufficient space and room for the next generation of leaders. More importantly, the job for the next generation of leaders deems to be simple, that is, they only need to undo what the previous generation did wrong.

REFERENCES

[1] Adams, B. (1913). *The theory of social revolutions*. Project Gutenberg EBook #10613 http://www.gutenberg.org/files/10613 /10613-h/ 10613-h.htm

[2] Abbott, J. (1848). *Charles I*. The Baldwin Project. http://www.mainlesson.com/display.php?author=abbottandbook=charles1andstory=_contents

[3] http://en.wikipedia.org/wiki/Alternate_history

[4] Thucydides. *The History of the Peloponnesian War*. Project Gutenberg Ebook #7142 http://www.gutenberg.org/cache/ epub/ 7142/pg7142.txt

[5] http://en.wikipedia.org/wiki/Cultural_Revolution

[6] http://threekingdoms.com/002.htm and http://threekingdoms.com /003.htm

[7] http://en.wikipedia.org/wiki/Great_Chinese_Famine

[8] http://threekingdoms.com/073.htm

[9] Blair, T. (2010). *A Journey: My Political Life*. Nee York: Knopf.

[10] Abbott, J. (1849). *Alexander the Great*. The Baldwin Project. http://www.mainlesson.com/display.php?author=abbottandbook=alexanderandstory=_contents

[11] Dodge, M.M. (1865). *Hans Brinker or The Silver Skates*. A free ebook from http://manybooks.net/

[12] Wu, G. (2009). *China: Has the Last Opportunity Passed by?!* New York: Nova Science Publishers.

[13] Schoenhals, M. (1996). *China's Cultural Revolution, 1966-1969: Not a Dinner Party*. NY: Armonk M.E. Sharpe.

[14] Giles, H.A. (1902). *China and the Chinese*. MA: Norwood Press J.S. Cushing and Co. – Berwick and Smith Norwood.

[15] Abbott, J. (1849). *Hannibal.* The Baldwin Project. http://www.mainlesson.com/display.php?author=abbottandbook=hannibalandstory=_contents

[16] Lu, X. (2006). *A Jin - Essays written in a Pavilion of Concession.* Beijing: People's Literature Publisher (in Chinese).

[17] Abbott, J (1857). *Richard I.* The Baldwin Project. http://www.mainlesson.com/display.php?author=abbottandbook=richard1andstory=_contents

[18] Abbott, J (1848). *Charles I.* The Baldwin Project. http://www.mainlesson.com/display.php?author=abbottandbook=charles1andstory=_contents

[19] http://en.wikipedia.org/wiki/Positive_feedback

[20] http://threekingdoms.com/046.htm

[21] Roosevelt, T. (2002). *Theodore Roosevelt, An Autobiography.* Project Gutenberg Ebook #3335.

[22] Dumas, A. (1998). *The Count of Monte Cristo.* Project Gutenberg Ebook #1184.

INDEX